# ORAL NARRATIVES AND THE AO-NAGAS

## A JOURNEY OF IDENTITY CONSTRUCTION

*Oral Narratives and the Ao-Nagas: A Journey of Identity Construction* explores the rich oral traditions of the Ao- Naga people, offering an exploration of their culture, identity, and worldview. Rooted in a vibrant storytelling tradition passed down through generations, this collection preserves folktales, myths, and personal accounts that reflect the Ao-Nagas' deep connection to their community, environment, and spiritual beliefs. Through meticulously gathered narratives, the book uncovers themes of identity construction, migration, and societal values. It highlights how these stories, steeped in motifs of transformation, kinship, and interconnection with nature, serve as powerful tools for cultural preservation and self-expression. Drawing on extensive fieldwork and analysis, the book provides readers with an intimate look at the social dynamics, gender roles, and spiritual cosmology of the Ao-Naga people. More than a collection of stories, *Oral Narratives and the Ao-Nagas* invites readers to experience the essence of Ao-Naga life, their struggles, triumphs, and the ever-evolving identity of a people navigating the complexities of history, modernity, and globalization. Perfect for scholars and storytellers alike, this book bridges cultural divides and celebrates the enduring power of oral tradition.

**Resenmenla Longchar** is an Assistant Professor of History at ICFAI University Nagaland with a Ph.D. from the University of Hyderabad. Her research focuses on Northeast Indian tribal cultures, oral traditions, gender roles, and identity construction. An accomplished scholar, she has published extensively on topics including Ao-Naga folklore, rituals, and community systems. Dr Longchar is deeply committed to preserving and analysing indigenous knowledge systems, offering fresh insights into the cultural and historical narratives of Northeast India.

# ORAL NARRATIVES AND THE AO-NAGAS

## A JOURNEY OF IDENTITY CONSTRUCTION

Resenmenla Longchar

http://www.highlanderpress.org

**Highlander Press**
9 Main St Hill
Dexter, Maine 04930
United States of America



ISBN: 979-8-9879339-1-6
Library of Congress Control Number: 2025939904

Cover image by Harshad Marathe
Design and layout by Highlander Press
Typeset in Gaudy Old Style by Prepress Plus Technologies
Printed in India

# CONTENTS

# FORWARD

Oral literature/tradition comprises folktales, folklores, folksongs, myths, proverbs, dances, festivals, myths, legends, fairy tales, etc. It is expressed in story forms which include stories of experiences — stories of love and revenge, justice and injustice, life and death, stories of celebration, hope and despair, and stories of struggle and freedom. They serve as the source for indigenous peoples' history, religious beliefs, social ethos and mores, and cultural milieu. Oral literature also serves as one of the most valuable sources of information about people, their lifestyles, belief systems, and their experiences of manifestations of supernatural powers. Therefore, stories are texts, foundations, and authoritative literature for the indigenous people. They are indigenous peoples' scripture and creed. These oral literatures shape our societies.

There is a difference between oral and literate culture in terms of daily life experiences and interpretation. While the indigenous stories are grounded in sound, natural objects, events, land, and environment, literate societies are grounded on sight, print, and historical events. For the indigenous societies, folk stories are sacred, and they do not need to be subjected to scientific investigation to discern their truth. If we apply modern scientific methods of analysis while interpreting the indigenous folk stories and myths, their true meaning tends to dissipate. But in many literate societies, truth must be subjected to scientific methods of analysis. If not, they are just superficial fairy tales. One should not apply modern scientific method while interpreting folk stories.

There is also a sharp difference between oral and literate societies in interpreting stories. A peculiar characteristic of indigenous peoples' stories is that they do not have an individual author. Oral literature/tradition is a collective creation of the folk. In the case of a literate society, a scholar writes stories. For indigenous peoples, the interpreters of the stories are the folk themselves (no experts needed), but in the case of literate societies, people have to depend on the experts to interpret for them. In the case of indigenous peoples, stories are common people's property and the folk themselves control them, but in the case of literate societies, experts and scholars control stories. Indigenous peoples' stories are never static or fixed. They undergo changes according to the context, performance and audience. On the contrary, stories are generally fixed in a literate society because they are written and documented.

However, oral experience is not without its limitations. Like literacy, orality is a two-edged sword. It can be oppressive or liberating. The responsibility of indigenous people, regardless of context, is to recognize the ways in which oral experience affects a certain community's understanding of the God-world-human relationship and to evaluate the fruits of such an understanding. This evaluation can lead to the practical application of moral values in the fields of justice, peace-making, and the creation of an inclusive community of all and for all.

Applying the indigenous method of interpretation in conversation with modern scholarship, Dr. Resenmenla Longchar has developed a methodology to reinterpret indigenous folklore, especially Ao-Naga folklore. I hope this well-articulated scholarly work of Dr. Longchar will enable readers to understand the deeper meaning of indigenous peoples' worldviews. I trust that all research scholars will find this book resourceful.

Prof. Wati Longchar
Regional Consultant for Theological Education in South & East Asia
International Ministries-American Baptist Churches & Ao Baptist
Arogo Mungdang
(IM-ABC & ABAM)

# PREFACE

Naga culture, in general, and Ao-Naga culture, in particular, are rooted in oral folklore traditions passed down through generations due to the absence of written records. Consequently, the primary source of narrative inquiry is the storyteller. During my investigation, I observed that the Ao-Nagas are exceptional narrators. Every vocal expression of their culture is deeply intertwined with their communal life experiences.

The goal of this book is to guide tribal communities in general, and the Ao-Nagas specifically, in constructing their identities through narratives. Narrators develop a 'narrative identity' through the process of interpretation, enabling them to establish both personal and social identities through their stories.

This book aims to help readers:
  i. Understand how oral narratives can serve as a valuable source of knowledge.
  ii. Grasp the concept of identity within the context of Ao-Naga folklife and its historical background.
  iii. Learn about the community's origins, migration, ecology, and lore, which distinguish them among Nagaland's indigenous tribes.

# ACKNOWLEDGEMENTS

First and foremost, I would like to express my heartfelt gratitude to God for the blessings and guidance throughout this journey. God's timing is always perfect.

I am deeply indebted to Dr. Michael T. Heneise and Highlander Press, whose unwavering support and encouragement have been instrumental in bringing this book to fruition. Your dedication to excellence and your commitment to this work's success have been invaluable, and I am immensely grateful for your guidance.

I am also profoundly grateful to my PhD supervisor, Dr. P.S. Kanaga Durga, and Dr. Y.A. Sudhakar Reddy, whose expertise and encouragement have been instrumental in shaping this work. Your insightful feedback and constant support have motivated me to strive for excellence, and I consider myself fortunate to have had you as mentors.

I am immensely grateful to Dr. Wati Longchar for graciously accepting the role of writing the foreword for this book. Your generosity in sharing your time and expertise is deeply appreciated.

This book owes its richness to the contributions of the cultural participants who shared their oral histories, folktales, and cultural knowledge during the research process. Their narratives, wisdom, and willingness to engage have provided a foundation for this study. I would like to particularly acknowledge individuals from various villages who made this possible: Otsufuba Longkumer and Longrichila Longchar from Longkhum village; Chubameren Jamir, Imolemba Jamir, and Imkongakum Imsong from Ungma village; Rev. Pona Jamir and R. Nungshimeren Ozukum from Mopongchuket village; Tsükdinungba Longkumer and Imtilepzuk Jamir from Changtongya village; and others, including Marla Longkumer, Sentinungla Longkumer, T. Kumzuk Ao, L. Teka Longchar, Dr. Purtongzuk Longchar, and K. Jamir. Regrettably, some of these esteemed respondents have now passed away, and I honor their memory and legacy with deep respect and gratitude.

To my family and friends, I am thankful for your unwavering belief in my abilities and steadfast support. Your prayers, love, encouragement, and understanding have been a continuous source of inspiration and strength. I am truly blessed to have such remarkable individuals in my life.

A special acknowledgment goes to my sister, Dr. Imchasenla, for her exceptional dedication to proofreading this book and providing valuable input. Your attention to detail and thoughtful suggestions have significantly enhanced the final product. I am immensely grateful for the time and effort you invested in making this book the best it can be.

Finally, I extend my thanks to everyone who has supported me throughout this journey, whether intellectually, emotionally, or creatively. Each contribution, no matter how small, has played a role in shaping this book. Your belief in me and your efforts to ensure this work's success mean more to me than words can express.

This book stands as a testament to the collective efforts of so many remarkable individuals. I am forever indebted to each of you for being part of this journey and for making this achievement possible.

# 1

# INTRODUCTION

The Ao culture is rooted in their folklore traditions transmitted orally throughout the generations since they have no written source. Oral narratives are dynamic genres that capture the essence of culture, including how it is experienced, portrayed, and passed down to future generations. Narratives are stories that have been passed down through generations as a means of communication, education, cultural preservation, and instilling knowledge and values. As a result, people adapt narratives to shape and understand their experiences, resulting in stories that are nothing more than their experiential expressions. Narratives are powerful tools used to convey stories in a structured and chronological manner through verbal communication. They serve to make sense of personal experiences and convey messages through diverse characters. This method of storytelling focuses on the lives and experiences of individuals, as well as the process of gathering research data through narrative means. At the core of narrative inquiry is the storyteller themselves, as people's lives are inherently made up of stories. These stories can be personal anecdotes or accounts of others' lives, all open to interpretation. The relationship between the storyteller and the listener, or the researcher and the respondent, greatly influences how these narratives are understood and shared. Through dialogue and communication, a narrator shares their experiences or recounts stories to others. This process of storytelling not only captures events but also conveys emotions, perspectives, and insights. Ultimately, narratives serve as a powerful tool for understanding and connecting with others through the art of storytelling.

Narrative creation is a dialogical process between the narrator's ego and the researcher. By embracing the dialogical method, which is reflexive, self-emanating, and emergent, valuable narratives and data are gathered in the field. This approach results in a rich corpus of thick data[1] that is co-created through dialogue between the ethnographer and the informant, blurring traditional distinctions between subject and object, researcher and informant. The reciprocal exchange of ideas fosters self-reflective knowledge production on both sides. The dialogical method serves as a powerful tool for researchers seeking to gain a deeper understanding of human reality. Despite initially having little to no shared experiences, fieldworkers and informants gradually develop a shared awareness of the activities unfolding around them through ongoing conversations. Narrative research not only guides the study process and informs data collection, but also contributes to the refinement of objective research techniques. In some cases, narrative inquiry can serve as the primary means of assessing real-world situations. In essence, narrative inquiry offers a methodological framework for exploring and making sense of personal experiences. Through thoughtful engagement with narratives, researchers can uncover valuable insights that contribute to a more nuanced understanding of the complexities of human existence.

In general, human life experiences and events lack a narrative framework until they are recounted. When narrators organise and convey their experiences in alignment with their sense of self, the resulting narratives create a rich framework of interpretations. Through this process, narrators develop a narrative identity that allows them to establish personal and social connections through their stories. Because the narrators' experiential expressions are regarded averted or subverted, the tales mirror the structure and cultural values of the society in which they are told and assimilated (Durga, 2007, 1). As a

---

[1] Clifford Geertz, 1973, *Thick Description: Toward an Interpretive Theory of Culture*, in The Interpretation of Cultures, New York: Basic Books, pp. 15-18

result, the narrative structure remains consistent with the thoughts of the narrators, which are shaped by the norms of their society. The social functions of these narratives, along with the cultural norms and laws of their social hierarchy, continue to play a significant role. The structure, function, and interpretation of folk narratives all contribute to the formation of the tellers' identities, both individually and collectively.

The Ao-Nagas are renowned for their storytelling abilities, with every narrative rooted in their community's life experiences. The narrators are influenced by the conventions, values, beliefs, and customary laws of their respective social groups, which are reflected in their storytelling. When examining Ao-Naga oral narratives, particularly folktales, one can observe consistent lifestyle patterns in both reality and expression.

Folklife is an extension of the boundaries of folklore. It is the people's traditional expressive culture, which is shared among numerous social groupings such as family, ethnic, occupational, religious, and regional organisations. Custom, belief, technical skill, language, theatre, ritual, architecture, music, play, dance, drama, ritual, pageantry, and craftsmanship all fall under the umbrella of expressive culture.[2] Folklife encompasses all of the oral traditions that have been passed down through the generations. Folklife is widespread, encompassing the changes and continuities of these traditions that occur in many aspects of people's lives and define folk groups' identities.

Identity is built on a foundation of consistency. Richard Jenkins (1996, 4) holds that the identity does not just exist but must always be established by the people and the community. Different genres of folklife construct and continue the identities of people as 'a member of a particular group' and 'as a group' throughout the generations despite changes in different spheres of their lives.

The Oxford Reference Dictionary defines 'identity' as the fact of being who or what a person or thing is, or a close similarity or feeling

---

[2] http://www.loc.gov/folklife/fieldwork/introduction.html. Accessed: 28 November 2011.

of understanding. According to the dictionary, the word 'identity' stems from the Latin root (*identitas*, from *idem*, 'the same') and has two basic meanings. The first is the concept of absolute sameness, identical to, and the second is the concept of distinctiveness or difference, which presumes consistency or continuity over time. Identity is a term used to describe a person's conception and expression of their individuality or group affiliations. Identity is an important concept that encompasses a person's sense of self and belonging to various groups. It plays a significant role in shaping our perceptions of ourselves and how we engage with the world. Our identity is a reflection of our beliefs, values, experiences, and relationships, and it is constantly evolving as we mature and evolves. Embracing and comprehending our identity is vital for personal development and fulfilment. Peter Robb (1997, 245–83) considers that identities are always multiple, contingent, and continuously constructed, so that traditions, also continually reinvented, are shared and reiterated practices and beliefs which reflect the collective memories of previous constructions. Thus, multiple identities operate at personal (individual), family level (relations), gender (social roles), sex (men and women), class and clan, community (a group of people), social (collective), global (worldwide), national, local, etc. In light of the above discussion, identity can broadly be categorised as personal and social.

Personal identity is a set of meanings that are linked to and preserve one's identity as a person; these self-meanings work in a variety of ways. A common system of meanings articulates both personal and role identities (Stets1995, 129–50). Individuals and groups are differentiated by their social identities in their interactions with other individuals and groups. It is the systematic development and meaning of relationships of similarity and difference between individuals, groups, and individuals and groups.

Temsula Ao (2006, 6–7) considers identity as a word loaded with meanings, evocative of multiple interpretations, and in today's context, implicated in a vociferous cry for an assertion. She believes that identity varies in terms of its spatial and temporal importance, and that it can gain or lose meaning. Identity for a Naga, particularly an Ao-Naga, is a multi-layered notion. Her Ao-Naga identity is divided into three categories: existential, locational, and artefactual. The Nagas' existential identity is enmeshed in mythological history about how they came to be, where they came from, and why they came to dwell in different areas or inhabit the geographical area known as Nagaland, as well as some places in neighbouring states. The Naga's geographical identity is rooted in the village where he or she was born and raised. This is due to the fact that this identity is defined by a specific ethnic and linguistic region. She claims that art, in all of its forms, never existed in the Naga environment for the sake of art. Whatever art forms are now associated with or allocated to the 'Naga' are descended from utilitarian things. Others provide the artefactual identity for her, but she does not construct it. She is concerned that, as a result of the production of hybridised cultural products for exchange in the business world, globalisation is combining the Ao-Naga identities. However, the failure of the author to recognise two specific points on Ao-Naga identity is evident viz., (i) culture is not static and changes according to changing needs of the people in time and space and (ii) the hybrid cultural products do not dehumanise and de-identify the traditional forms, but construct 'new identities' and create 'new contexts' for their sustenance and continuity, thus renewing the Folklife of the society.

Alan Dundes (1989, 4) interprets that the folklore marks the identity of its respective folk groups. He highlights the importance of identity in understanding that it is impossible to speak about sameness without mentioning difference, because if all members of a given set were identical and the set was equal to the universe, sameness would be meaningless. In order for an individual to establish a distinct identity, they must differentiate themselves from others. As a result, folk groups develop esoteric and exoteric expressive behaviour to represent their own 'self' as well as the self of the 'other', and thus construct identities as members of the folk group (personal identity) on the one hand, and as a folk group (group identity) on the other, which can be distinguished from other social groups in a given geographical space. Thus, the totality of folklife, as represented in their lore and lifestyle patterns, speaks about how folk groups remain persistent and consistent in holding on to their identities, at least symbolically, in changing times.

The book is structured into five chapters that examine the significance of oral narratives within the Ao culture, highlighting their crucial role in transmitting traditions and shaping identity. It will explore how these narratives serve as a powerful tool for communication, education, and cultural preservation, reflecting the rich experiences and values of the community. The book will explore into the intricate structure and typology of Ao-Naga narratives, examining how they encapsulate the core strands of identity and social values. Furthermore, the book will touch upon the multi-layered nature of identity for the Ao-Naga people. Overall, the book sheds light on the complex relationship between oral narratives and the construction of identity within the Ao-Naga community. *Introduction* discusses the relevance of oral narrative, how narratives become a source of study, and how many genres of folklife construct and continue people's identities. *Chapter 2: Tales from the Highlands: Narratives of the Ao-Nagas* incorporates forty narratives gathered from the Ao-Nagas which are used as crucial source material in the next two chapters. *Chapter 3: Origin and Dispersal of Nagas: A Folkloric Perspective* discusses the migration and origin myths of the Nagas in general, and the Ao-Nagas in particular. The Ao-Nagas' views on their origin is also discussed. *Chapter 4: Ao-Naga Narrative Typology and Structure: Metaphors of Identity*, examines (i) how the Ao-Nagas' oral narratives (both personal and folk) maintain their core strands of identity in their narrative motifs and themes, and (ii) how the oral narratives' structures reflect the Ao-Nagas' social stratification and cultural values. In this chapter, folk narratives are examined using the paradigms of Proppian and Lévi-Straussian structural models, as well as Derridean post-structural hermeneutical discourse and narrative inquiry. Chapter 5, our final chapter is the *conclusion*.

# 2

# TALES FROM THE HIGHLANDS: NARRATIVES OF THE AO-NAGAS

Humans possess an innate inclination to share narratives, as storytelling is widely recognised as a fundamental mode of self-expression. Narratives are the sole routes via which one can speak with the other over the generations, especially in oral societies like the Ao-Nagas, where communication and transmission of knowledge is reliant on orality and mnemonics. Narrators find meaning in their own lives, as well as in the cultures and environments in which they were born and raised, by telling stories. When folktales are examined closely, they reflect similar lifestyle tendencies in both reality and expression. Folktales are stories that are passed down from generation to generation through word of mouth. There is no single author for true folktales. They change throughout time when different people tell them different things. As a result, they are works of 'the folk' or the people. The narratives were collected through fieldwork conducted in various villages in the Ao culture. The Ao culture is deeply rooted in folklore traditions that have been passed down orally through generations, as there are no written sources available. The primary focus of this chapter is to utilise oral narratives as the main source of information. Men and women from different socio-economic backgrounds and age groups were the main participants in the field study. The research was carried out in villages such as Longkhum, Ungma, Mopongchuket, and Changtongya, as well as in the Mokokchung and Dimapur districts. Prior to entering the field, I thoroughly familiarised myself with the literature on the area and its people, studying the geography, weather conditions, and locations. This preparation helped me to effectively engage with the local community and gather valuable information for the study. Focus group discussions were held with members of councils and elders of folk groups to collect narratives and insights on various issues. Both directive and non-directive interviews were conducted, using open-ended questions to gain a deeper understanding of the community's perspective. By engaging with the local community and utilising various research methods, valuable insights have been gained that will contribute to a better understanding of this unique culture. Overall, utilising the narratives, the following chapters aim to offer a thorough analysis of the Ao culture by examining into their oral traditions and narratives. Throughout my fieldwork experience, I struggled with various challenges, especially when consulting with the informants for their narratives. One limitation was that many informants struggled to recall folktales from memory because they had stopped sharing folktales and viewed them simply as stories for children. To tackle this problem, I started giving advance notice to my informants about my impending visits, giving them the chance to remember the traditional stories. Despite putting in a great deal of effort, the stories gathered lacked the intricate details I desired because of the informants' limited memory. Contrarily, the informants indicated a penchant for conversing about *sobaliba*3 over folktales. *Sobaliba* would essentially mean an ethics of living with regards to the society, culture, tradition, environment, nature, etc., which is required in the day to day living of an individual's life, be it to self or to the community. Overall, despite encountering limitations in the fieldwork process, my observations showed that the informants shared anecdotes with

---

[3] "The concept of Sobaliba - from the outside looking in": https://nagalandpost. com/index.php/2019/05/03/the-concept-of-sobaliba-from-the-outside-looking-in/. Accessed 29 February 2024

happiness and laughter. Occasionally, they enacted scenes, prompting a wave of nostalgia as they reflected on their youth spent immersed in the stories shared by their parents and grandparents.

This chapter contains documentation of forty Ao-Naga folk narratives that serves as the main source of information and are set to be examined extensively in the next two chapters.

## NARRATIVE 1: THE ORIGIN MYTH OF THE NAGAS: TIGER, SPIRIT, AND MAN[4]

Once upon a time, there lived the first woman named *Dzülümosüro*, which means 'purest water' or 'crystal clear water'. She resided in an area known as *Makhrüfü* or Makhel, where one day she was found resting under a tree with her legs wide apart. It was during this time that she became pregnant, as a cluster of clouds passed over her and some drops of liquid fell onto her private parts. *Dzülümosüro* went on to give birth to three children: a tiger, a spirit, and a man (human being). As their mother grew older and weaker, the three brothers took turns caring for her. However, it was only when the Man cared for his mother that she felt at ease, as he treated her with the utmost care and concern. The tiger and the spirit, on the other hand, caused her anxiety and discomfort. The mother's health continued to decline, and as her end approached, the sons began to fight over her land inheritance. In order to resolve the issue without bloodshed, the mother devised a competition for her sons. She threw a grass ball into the air and declared that whoever touched it first would inherit the land. Knowing her children's strengths and weaknesses, she guided the man to use a bow and arrow to claim victory. Following her advice, the man successfully shot the ball and secured the property. The tiger,

---

[4] Amongst the forty collected narratives, this tale is the only one that was not collected by the author. Rather it is extracted from a printed publication titled "The Origin of Tiger, Spirit, and Humankind: A Mao Naga Myth" by X. P. Mao, NEHU, Shillong, *Indian Folklife*, Serial No.33, July 2009.

feeling defeated, fled into the woods, while the spirit disappeared in another direction of *kashüpü* (south). The mother's wish for her property to be passed down to her clever and prudent son was fulfilled, as the man proved himself to be worthy of her trust.

## NARRATIVE 2: MYTH OF FLAT STONE AND THREE BROTHERS[5]

Once upon a time, a man named Koza journeyed from the east and found himself in Mekhroma (Makhel, Manipur region). Pausing to contemplate his next move, he sought guidance from a higher power. To his surprise, a bird alighted on his *mithun's* horn and then flew off towards Khezhakeno. Koza dropped a stick to the ground to confirm the bird's direction, and it aligned perfectly with the bird's flight path. Taking this as a sign, Koza continued his journey to Khezhakeno. Upon reaching his destination, Koza witnessed the same bird perched on a stone slab. Intrigued, he observed a frog dropping a grain of rice onto the stone, which miraculously doubled in size. Inspired by this phenomenon, Koza poured a basket of rice onto the slab, and the grains multiplied before his eyes. With this newfound fortune, Koza decided to settle in the Khezhakeno region, where he was eventually blessed with three sons. The sons, aware of the stone's mystical powers, began spreading their paddy on the slab daily, witnessing the grains multiply. However, a dispute arose among them over this duty, causing concern for their parents. In an attempt to rid the stone of its spirit and resolve the conflict, the parents resorted to drastic measures. They broke eggs, covered the stone with bush-wood, and set it ablaze, causing the stone to shatter with a deafening crack. As the spirit ascended to heaven in a cloud of smoke, the stone lost its miraculous abilities. The three sons, now ancestors of the Angami, Lotha, and Sumi Naga tribes, departed, while the parents remained in Kezami villages, becoming

[5] Tsükdinungba Longkumer (male, 75 years old, Changtongya village), oral narration, April 24, 2008.

the forefathers of the Khezha clan of the Chakhesang Naga tribe. To this day, the Angamis still point to the large, cracked stone.

## NARRATIVE 3: LIJABA AND HIS CREATION[6]

*Lijaba* is revered as the supreme god and the creator of the earth. He made the earth to be very beautiful, smooth, and plain. However, during the creation process, a water cockroach known as *tsü leplo* suddenly appeared and falsely warned *Lijaba* of approaching enemies wielding dao and spear, before disappearing just as quickly. Fearing for the safety of his creation, *Lijaba* hastily completed the formation of the Ao country in a rushed and disorganised manner. As a result of this hurried creation, the Aos believe that their region is characterised by an abundance of mountains and hills, with fewer picturesque plains, valleys, and rivers compared to the neighbouring Assam region. The land of Assam is described as flat and the habitat of the Nagas is depicted as hilly.

## NARRATIVE 4: THE ATTACK ON KUBOK VILLAGE[7]

In a time long past, there resided a young married man named Shiluti. One fateful day, while out hunting, he stumbled upon a narrow path that piqued his curiosity. Eager to explore its origins and destination, Shiluti embarked on a journey down the mysterious trail. After a lengthy trek, he encountered a blockade of fully grown cane trees obstructing his path. Noticing sharp sticks nearby, typically used for clearing shrubs, Shiluti took it upon himself to painstakingly remove the obstacles hindering

[6] Otsufuba Longkumer (male, 73 years old, Longkhum village), oral narration, December 18, 2007. This narration is also mentioned by J.P. Mills in his book *The Ao Nagas* (Mills, 1926, p. 220). In his version, the water cockroach is a water-beetle.
[7] Otsufuba Longkumer (male, 73 years old, Longkhum village), oral narration, December 18, 2007.

his progress. Upon successfully clearing the path, Shiluti continued his exploration the following day, eventually reaching the end of the trail. From this vantage point, he beheld the settlement of Kubok nestled on the slopes of the valley. It dawned on him that this was the very location where the village's search party8 had discovered the headless bodies of those who had ventured into the forest. Returning home, Shiluti shared the unsettling discovery with his wife, unaware that their conversation had been overheard by locals. Word quickly spread to the village elders, prompting them to convene a meeting and summon Shiluti to provide a detailed account of his findings. Reluctant at first, Shiluti ultimately acquiesced, recognising the importance of complying with the council's directives. During the meeting, the council instructed Shiluti to bring a *dao* and recount his observations. It was unanimously decided that an attack on the Kubok settlements was necessary. Shiluti was entrusted with the task of training and assessing the village warriors who would partake in the assault. In a ceremonial display of readiness, Shiluti slaughtered a healthy pig and divided it into thirty pieces, which were then cast into a blazing fire. Twenty-nine trainees, following Shiluti's lead, retrieved a burning piece of meat and held it in their mouths. Consequently, they were all well-equipped to confront their adversaries. The Mongsen Aos suffered defeat when they launched an attack on Kubok village. Subsequently, the Chungli Aos compelled the Mongsen Aos to relocate to Chungliyimti and establish a *khel*. They have remained united ever since.

## NARRATIVE 5: CHILD OF SUN AND MOON[9]

Once upon a time, there was a husband and wife who resided in a quaint village. One day, while the wife was diligently drying grains on

[8] The smart, strong and depended warriors were selected by the village elders in the search party.
[9] Tsükdinungba Longkumer (male, 75 years old, Changtongya village), oral narration, April 24, 2008.

the balcony (*sunglang*), she suddenly fainted, enveloped in darkness. This incident marked a turning point in their relationship, as there had been no sexual intercourse between them prior to this event. Upon regaining consciousness, the wife questioned her husband if he had been present on the balcony at the time of her fainting. His response was in the negative, denying any involvement. The wife, attributing her condition to the mysterious darkness, expressed her concerns about the impact it may have on her unborn child. Despite her apprehensions, she eventually gave birth to a remarkable child, who exhibited exceptional qualities and a unique character. This child became the progenitor of a new clan, heralding a new chapter in their family's history.

## NARRATIVE 6: THE STORY OF LONGKONGLA[10]

Longkongla was a righteous woman who lived in Chungliyimti village once upon a time. She was a member of the Longkumer family. She was a just and upright woman who was hospitable and loved children and everyone on the earth. A male hornbill (*tenem ozü*) passed her by one day as she was weaving her cloth in her courtyard. "*I wish the hornbill dropped one of its feathers so that I can wear it to the Moatsü festival*", she wished at the time. The hornbill then let go of one of its feathers. She was pleased when she saw the feather. The feather remained in her *kettsu* (cane mat box). She discovered the next day that the feather had transformed into a sharpening stone. She kept the stone in the fore room at the entrance to her house. That stone was soon converted into a shattered bamboo basin. She tossed it out the window. She realised the broken bamboo basin had transformed into a baby boy later that night. He was in tears. She raised him as a

---

[10] Sakunungla Longkumer (female, 55 years old, Longkhum village), oral narration, June 18, 2008. A similar story is narrated by the Chang Nagas. In that story, the name of the woman is Chimendangla (Anungla Longkumer, 2017, pp.197–199).

foster child and gave him the name *Pongtang*, which means "the one whom everyone attempts to carry".

He matured into a strong and handsome young man who was admired by all women, young and old. Some of the villagers were jealous of the boy. He was taken fishing one day and was killed. After learning of the tragedy, Longkongla resolved to exact vengeance by killing all of the residents. She intended to kill the children first, then the villagers who would come to her house seeking vengeance. She killed a huge pig and cooked it one day when all the people were out in the field. She invited all of the children to the feast. She closed the doors and set fire to it while they were eating. Except for one boy who fled and informed the village, all of the children were burned to death. When word of the tragedy reached the village's chief (*ungr*), the council ordered all of his villagers to stay at home and execute Longkongla. After learning of their plan, she surrounded herself with grains – rice, millet, soybeans, and maize – and waited for the villagers to arrive while weaving her cloth. All of the men later met with their *dao* (machete). They slipped on the rice grains and beans as they approached her with the dao and fell. As a result, Longkongla killed everyone with her sword, a weaver's baton (*alem*). She was alone by the time nightfall arrived. She couldn't live on her own. She asked the god of heaven (*anintsüngba*) to lift her to heaven as she no longer wished to remain on earth. The god told her that he would lift her to heaven only if she forgot all her attachments, possessions, and belongings on the earth. Moreover, she could not look down even if her kith and kin called for her. God further told her that if she did not follow these conditions she would be dropped from heaven. She promised him that she would not to look down. The god stretched the rope from heaven to lift her. But halfway to heaven, she heard all the cries of her cows, dogs, pigs, chickens, and goats. As their voices grew louder she looked down because she missed them. The moment she looked down she was dropped to the earth and turned into a rock. Her son who was born from a hornbill feather became the originator of the *Ozukumer* clan of the Aos.

## NARRATIVE 7: THE STORY OF THE REVENGEFUL SONS (*MANG YANGBA JABASO*)[11]

In the village of Koridang, there resided a family consisting of a mother and her two sons. Tragically, when the sons were young, their father was killed by members of the Sangtam tribe who also took the dead body of the father. As the sons grew older, they yearned for answers about their father's fate, prompting them to repeatedly question their mother. Her response was always the same - to wait until they were mature enough to handle the truth. Upon reaching the ages of twelve and thirteen, the mother decided it was time to reveal the identity of their father's killer. She instructed her sons to sharpen their *daos*, a type of large machete used as a weapon, and presented them with a challenge. If they could cut a dried cane rope in one swift motion, she would disclose the name of the perpetrator. The sons successfully completed the task, leading their mother to disclose the entire story of their father's demise. Following their mother's guidance, the sons infiltrated the killer's household under the guise of offering their services. They gained his trust over the years, patiently waiting for the opportune moment to exact their revenge. When the time came, they lured the old man to a fishing trip and ultimately ended his life in the forest. Through their mother's wisdom and their own patience and determination, the sons were able to avenge their father's death and eliminate their lifelong enemy. The tale of their journey from grief to justice serves as a testament to the power of perseverance and strategic thinking.

[11] Tsükdinungba Longkumer (male, 75 years old, Changtongya village), oral narration, April 24, 2008.

## NARRATIVE 8: SARILONGLI AND HIS WIFE[12]

Once upon a time, Sarilongli and his wife resided in a village where the daily tasks of working in the fields, cooking, fetching water, and gathering firewood had become mundane and tiresome. Yearning for a place where they could live without the burden of labour, they embarked on a journey that lasted several days. Eventually, they reached a location known as "*Alikodaktsür*". Upon their arrival, they encountered individuals of diminutive stature who were diligently collecting seeds from a short plant known as *likok dong*. These seeds possessed a tangy flavour, which intrigued Sarilongli and his wife. However, they soon realised their folly and returned to their village with a newfound perspective. Addressing the villagers, Sarilongli and his wife imparted a valuable lesson, that true prosperity and contentment could not be achieved without hard work and dedication. The villagers, in turn, were grateful for the couple's insight and embraced the importance of labour in their own lives. From that day forward, Sarilongli and his wife lived harmoniously, supporting each other and finding joy in their daily tasks. They never again complained about their work, understanding that diligence and cooperation were the keys to a fulfilling existence.

## NARRATIVE 9: TSÜPOSANG[13]

Once upon a time, there was *Tsüposang*. He was very friendly with all living beings in the forest and also in the waters. Since he knew the language of the animals, he could locate them wherever they are. Whenever he wanted his food — a bird, or a fish, or any other animal

---

[12] Imolemba Jamir (male, 57 years old, Ungma village), oral narration, December 19, 2007.

[13] Imolemba Jamir (male, 57 years old, Ungma village), oral narration, December 19, 2007.

meat — he used to take the best among them very casually to his home for his dinner. One day, his *anuk* (son-in-law) asked him, "*Oku* (uncle), let me also come to the jungle with you". *Tsüposang* frankly denied. He convinced him that "*when you watch the animals' behaviour, it will look funny and incomprehensible to you. If a new person like you makes any noise they will get disturbed or possibly frightened. They will no longer remain my friends and may run far away from me. Better do not come*". However, as the son-in-law pestered, he accepted to take him to the forest on the condition that he would not open his mouth. Finally, they reached the forest. *Tsüposang* began to converse with the animals by making some sounds to call animals. He began to call and talk to the animals by name like, "*Shitsü* (monkey) *kang kang, mesü* (deer) *kang kang*". Then all the animals and birds responded to him and gathered around him. The son-in-law who was hiding behind the trees saw a *chipcho* (porcupine)14 trying to climb up a tree. The attempts of such a short animal to climb up a tree seemed funny to the son-in-law. Therefore, he laughed loudly at it. All the birds and animals ran away after listening to his new voice and sounds and they were no more available to *Tsüposang* to pick them informally to home for food. He grew angry with his *anuk* for entering the forest and spoiling his friendship with the living beings in the forest world. Then, out of regret, he requested the animals and birds, "*Please, keep at least a leg or a hand of the porcupine on the pathway for me*". A jackal passing by that way overheard his request and conveyed to the animals, "*grandfather has told us to keep at least your faeces (sü) on the pathway for him*". From that time onward, the Ao-Nagas find the faeces of the animals in every pathway but not the bodily remains of the porcupine.

---

14 This animal lives in the deep forest and difficult to hunt down. For the Ao-Nagas the quill/spike of the porcupine served many purposes — as earrings, as a means to make hair bun strong, used in weaving, and to part the hairs on the head. The meat of the animal is used as a medicine.

## NARRATIVE 10: THE STORY OF PUNASOSANG[15]

Once upon a time, a young man named Punasosang from *Soyim* found himself enamoured with a girl from *Impang*, the upper *khel*. He would often visit her dormitory, known as *tsuki*, to spend time with her. One day, on his way to the dormitory, he came across a bird that had died due to the forceful winds. This sight left him feeling melancholic. As time went by, the villagers prepared to celebrate the *Moatsu* festival. Punasosang, along with the members of the upper boys' dormitory (*khel arju*), journeyed to the lower *khel* to secure a pig (*ak*) for the festivities. They purchased the pig from a widow for fifty tin (*yimchi*) of grains. On the day of the festival, the *arju* members slaughtered the pig at the widow's residence, and the villagers enjoyed a grand feast. Following the festival, it was time for the villagers to tend to their fields. The upper *khel* villagers were able to harvest their fields early and without much difficulty. However, the lower *khel* villagers faced challenges due to the hilly terrain of their field site, causing delays in their harvest. During a stroll through the lower *khel* after the harvest, Punasosang noticed the widow struggling to complete her work. He sought assistance from the *arju* members of the upper *khel*, and together they helped the widow finish her tasks. In gratitude, the widow blessed all the boys for their kindness and help.

## NARRATIVE 11: *ALUYIMER* (FARMER)[16]

Once upon a time, in the village of *Nujongkong*, there lived a widower named Sangmonger. He resided with his grandson, Talisangba. During

---

[15] Rev. L. Pona Jamir (male, 77 years old, Mopongchuket village), oral narration, May 24, 2008.

[16] L. Teka Longchar (male, 66 years old, Longkhum village), oral narration, June 13, 2008.

a period of drought, the villagers faced a severe water shortage as all rivers and streams had dried up. Fortunately, the widower and his grandson's field was located near a flowing river where the villagers used to catch fish to sell. One day, the grandson asked his grandfather if they should also go fishing like the other villagers. However, the wise widower remained silent and instructed his grandson to fetch water from the river to irrigate the field while he tended to the soil. On their way back from fishing, some villagers pushed the grandson, causing the widower to sing a song questioning the forces at play, "*Tayipti tentsu mopong asu jang mopong ako, apodaka nemtsung o talisangba ita nugoktsudima*" (What kind of wind is blowing this morning in our direction? What type of force is this, that Talisangba is being pushed in this way?). The following day, the grandson expressed his desire to go fishing again, but his grandfather promised to catch a big fish for him one day if he worked hard in the field. As harvest time approached, the villagers found their fields barren while the widower and his grandson reaped a bountiful harvest. After the harvest, the widower requested the villagers to bring him the biggest fish alive. In return, he gave them rice grains. He then served the fish to his grandson on a wooden platter covered with grains, emphasising the importance of hard work in the fields. Through this experience, the widower taught his grandson a valuable lesson about the rewards of effort and hard work. As the grandson played happily with the fish, the widower reminded him that those who work diligently in the fields will never lead an unhappy life, as grains can be exchanged for anything one desires.17

[17] There is an Ao proverb related to this story which says that somebody who just goes fishing ends up destitute. According to the narrator, the tale illustrates the importance of hard work and dedication, as exemplified by the widower and his grandson. It serves as a reminder that success and happiness are often the result of one's efforts and perseverance.

## NARRATIVE 12: THE BOY WITH SORES ON HIS BODY[18]

Once upon a time, in the village of Chungliyimti, there were two settlements known as the upper and lower *khels (mepu)*19, inhabited by the Chungli and Mongsen groups respectively. In the lower *khel* of the Mongsen group, there was a boy named Chungrongjung, who was considered the best among his peers. Unfortunately, he suffered from lesions all over his body due to a snake bite. Chungrongjung faced rejection and isolation from the villagers, including the girls he used to visit in the dormitory. Feeling dejected, he wandered into the forest and came across a snake with similar wounds. The villagers thrashed the snake with stones and daos. The snake approached a pond. It chewed some leaves and applied its paste to the wounds on its body. When the snake returned for leaves on the second day, the boy observed it. He observed the bruises cured. The snake returned on the third day as well, chewing and applying it to its body. All of the bruises had healed, and the skin had smoothed out. The boy noticed how the snake's wounds were healed and speculated that it might be a medicinal plant. He then took a few leaves from the tree. He chewed it and rubbed it to his body's wounds. All of the wounds gradually healed and became handsome in no time. When he returned to the village, the girls who had once rejected him now welcomed him with open arms, not recognising the once-afflicted boy. He told the girls that he didn't have any gold or silver to offer and wanted to sit near the firewood, which is where he used to sit when he had body sores. The girls then realised it was him who was covered in sores all over his body. They urged him to marry them, but he refused and departed. He eventually got rich and was able to purchase, maintain, and breed the animal *mithun*20, which

---

[18] Tsükdinungba Longkumer (male, 75 years old, Changtongya village), oral narration, April 24, 2008.

[19] Localities, sectors or wards in the village.

[20] The *mithun* (Bos frontalis), the domesticated free-range bovine species, is an important component of the livestock production system of North-Eastern hilly region of India. This unique bovine species is believed to be domesticated more than 8000 years ago. The *mithun* is primarily reared as a meat animal. It is also used as a ceremonial animal and plays important role in economic, social and

was the privilege of the wealthy. Nobody in the world, according to the forefathers, could breed as large a *mithun* as Chungrongjung.

## NARRATIVE 13: THE WIFE WHO RETURNED HOME[21]

Once upon a time, there was a married couple who had two sons. One day, the wife decided to take her sons to her father's house without any explanation. The husband, feeling frustrated by his wife's sudden departure, decided not to go after her and instead focused on his work in the fields and taking care of the pigs. Meanwhile, the wife began to feel lonely and longed to return home, but she couldn't bring herself to do so as she was the one who had left. Eventually, her desire to reunite with her husband grew too strong to ignore. Taking her sons with her, she made her way back to their home. Upon their arrival, the wife and her sons peeked through the door to find the husband busy preparing food for the pigs. "*Father!*" exclaimed the elder son, "*we're standing right here*". "Oh! Come into the home, why are you standing there?" the father exclaimed as soon as he heard that. That's how the wife got back home.

## NARRATIVE 14: THE TALE OF SAMATABA[22]

Once upon a time, in the village of Mopongchuket[23], there was a revered pond known as *awatsung*. This pond was believed to be home

cultural life. Besides, it is now established that superior quality milk and hide can be obtained from *mithuns*. Online source: http://www.nrcmithun.res.in/, accessed 13 December 2011.

[21] Longrichila Longchar (female, 78 years old, Longkhum village), oral narration, December 20, 2007.

[22] R. Nungshimeren Ozukum (male, 64 years old, Mopongchuket village), oral narration, June 26, 2008.

[23] This village is located in the Asetkong range.

to a powerful devil, whom the villagers would offer eggs, chicken, and pigs in exchange for protection from impending dangers. The devil's strength was such that it could even move cows from one place to another, forming alliances with villagers who would alert authorities in times of peril. One day, the peaceful existence of the village was threatened when the Ahoms from Assam arrived to attack. Despite taking a bath in the sacred pond and killing a dog for sustenance, the Ahoms were met with resistance from the devil, who instilled fear in them and drove them away under the cover of night. The villagers, empowered by the devil's protection, were able to chase and defeat the Ahoms, leaving behind their weapons in a tree trunk near the pond. This pond, once known as süngkotenep, held a significant place in the village's history. One day, as the villagers made their way to the fields, they encountered a large snake in a tree. Despite their efforts to kill it with spears, catapults, bows, and arrows, they were unsuccessful. It was at this moment that a young man named Samataba, who had been ostracised by the village council, stepped forward. Samataba, whose name meant 'the one who did not get meat' in the village of Chungtia, had journeyed to the Langpangkong range after being denied membership by the council. Despite the tradition that forbade new members from entering or leaving the village during times of conflict, Samataba was called upon to slay the snake. With a simple request, "*asa nüka meta, azü nüka meta, kü tenung samataba kü madang ko teplakzukang*" ("My name is Samataba, and I didn't receive any meat or rice beer. Come and fall before me") he used a catapult to defeat the snake, showcasing his bravery and skill.

## NARRATIVE 15: DISTRIBUTION OF PROPERTY[24]

Once upon a time, a wealthy family faced a tragic loss when the mother passed away, leaving her two daughters under the care of their

---

[24] Rev. L. Pona Jamir (male, 77 years old, Mopongchuket village), oral narration, May 24, 2008.

father, Tamayangba. Before her death, the mother entrusted many clothes, necklaces, and ornaments to Tamayangba for their daughters. As Tamayangba aged, he made the decision to divide his late wife's belongings between his daughters. However, he harboured concerns that his daughters would quarrel over their mother's estate once he passed away. To prevent any potential disputes, Tamayangba devised a clever plan. While his daughters were busy organising his memorial service, he feigned illness and pretended to be dead. The daughters, unaware of the trick, began mourning their father in the traditional manner of singing songs of praise. The eldest daughter sings to his father, "*Oh Apa Tamayangba yatem dangko kongto kongra den dang chowng nupasü*" ("Why are you leaving us, oh Father Tamayangba? You always wanted to eat dry meat in the evenings when you were alive"). The father then understood from the song of his eldest daughter that her mourning reflected more accusation rather than concern for him even in the matters of food. He then listened to the younger daughter's song. She sang, "*Father Tamayangba, when you cross Meyutsüngba's (Lord of justice) place, shout and go down saying, 'Yangrenmenla's (her name) father is coming down.*" Upon hearing his daughters' songs, Tamayangba realised the true extent of their feelings towards him. To their astonishment, he revealed himself to be alive and well after they had finished singing. He then proceeded to distribute his late wife's belongings to his daughters. Due to the elder daughter's disrespectful behaviour, the younger daughter received all the exquisite clothes and beautiful ornaments, while the elder daughter was left with the less desirable items.

## NARRATIVE 16: MENANGSANGLA AND NOKSHILOBA[25]

Once upon a time, there was a woman named *Menangsangla*. She was a well-known woman because of her ability to practice magic.

---

[25] Rev. L. Pona Jamir (male, 77 years old, Mopongchuket village), oral narration, May 24, 2008.

She was married to *Temjensoba*, but not so long after their marriage, he died leaving her to become a widow. In the village where she lived, there was a man named *Nokshiloba* who waited so long for *Menangsangla* because he wanted to marry her but unfortunately, she refused to live with him. This hurt him. One day, *Nokshiloba* did not go to the field. That day, he rolled a mat made of bamboo and hid the mat under the floor of *Menangsangla's* house. After that, he informed and raised an alarm to the villagers that he has lost his mat. The villagers who were in the village started to look for the mat. Later the mat was found in *Menangsangla's* house. The next day, she was called by the village elders. She was blamed by the elders as a thief for stealing the mat of *Nokshiloba*. She begged the elders not to call her a thief as she did not steal his mat, but the village elders did not listen to her plea since the mat was found at her house. After the case was over, in front of the village elders, *Menangsangla* told *Nokshiloba*, "*When you die, I will also die on the same day and both of us will be judged at Meyutsungba's place (god of judgment) to know whether I'm right or wrong*". Then she left the place. One day *Menangsangla* heard that *Nokshiloba* had died. Suddenly she also died on the same day, exactly as foretold by her. Even her granddaughter also died that day.

Her granddaughter rose from death within a short time and narrated one story like this, "*I died along with my grand-mother and Nokshiloba, so we all went together to Meyutsungba's place and reached at the same time. After that, Meyutsungba started to judge between grandmother and Nokshiloba by asking them to each throw a spear on a tree. Nokshiloba aimed and threw but was not able to touch the tree and broke his spear, whereas grandmother brought her anem (weaving tool), aimed at the tree and threw the anem with all her strength. It went straight and nailed itself on the tree. After the test was over, the god told them, 'when you two were alive on earth, you Nokshiloba called Menangsangla a thief but it is not true. Today, through the test, it is proven that Nokshiloba is wrong'*". This was the story told to the villagers by *Menangsangla's* granddaughter. After hearing the story, they came to realise that *Menangsangla* was telling the truth.

## NARRATIVE 17: THE DEVIL AND THE OLD MAN[26]

The story is said to have taken place when there was no difference between gods and men. This story took place before the village of Changtongya yimsen (previously called *Mangdangtakong*) was separated from Changtongya. There was an old man named Punazüngba. One day he went into the jungle to set *sang* (traps) to catch birds. After some time, he went to check the traps. To his surprise, instead of birds, he found a she-devil named *Oanglemla*[27] caught in the trap. When she saw the old man, she begged him, "*Old man, please do not kill me. I will bless you with good food until you die*'. But he refused and said, "*Oh devil, why should I spare you. I will kill you right now*". When the old man did not listen to her, she said again, "*Since you want to kill me, I will break your plate*[28] *too*". But the old man killed the devil and went back home. When he arrived home, he found that his daughter had died at home. When the devil said, "*I will break your plate*", she had meant that his daughter would die. He met his villagers and told them that he had killed *Oanglemla*. But they did not believe him, because according to their beliefs, no one could kill a devil. He wanted to prove them wrong and took them to the place where the devil had been killed. When they reached the place, all they found was the dried body of the devil. That is why the place was called *Mangdangtakong*, which means dried body.

[26] Tsükdinungba Longkumer (male, 75 years old, Changtongya village), oral narration, April 24, 2008.

[27] It is believed by the people that this is a devilish creature that lives in the jungle near a river or lake.

[28] The plate is metaphorically representing the daughter who takes care and prepares food for the father.

## NARRATIVE 18: THE CUSTOM OF DEBT-REPAYMENT[29]

In the village of Longkhum, there resided a family consisting of a father, two sons, and a daughter. However, tragedy struck when the father decided to divorce his wife, leaving his family with no inheritance. He then remarried a widow and moved into her home. Sadly, when the father passed away, his debts fell upon his first wife and their children. The ironic twist was that the new wife and her children from her previous marriage were not held responsible for repaying the debts accumulated by the second husband.

## NARRATIVE 19: THE RICH GIRL WHO BECAME A SPINSTER[30]

Once upon a time, in a village, resided a wealthy family with a beautiful daughter. Their wealthy lifestyle brought them much joy and comfort. The daughter, enamoured by a handsome but impoverished young man, found herself entangled in a forbidden love affair. However, upon learning of their relationship, the girl's parents scorned the boy, deeming him unworthy of their daughter due to his lack of wealth. Despite facing constant ridicule and insults from the girl's parents whenever he visited, the boy remained steadfast in his love for her. Eventually, he realised that their love was doomed due to her parents' disapproval. In a moment of despair, he informed his beloved that they could never be together, as her parents would never accept him. Determined to defy her parents and marry the man she loved, the girl remained resolute. However, her parents' relentless humiliation of the boy led him to devise a plan. At night, when all the villagers

[29] Sakunungla Longkumer (female, 55 years old, Longkhum village), oral narration, June 18, 2008.
[30] Sakunungla Longkumer (female, 55 years old, Longkhum village), oral narration, June 18, 2008.

were about to sleep, he went to his lover's house and called, *"Uncle, uncle, why are you closing your door? I came to your house to say a word, but since you don't want to open the door, let me just say this and go. I came to say that I won't be able to marry your daughter, let her get married to some other boy"*. After saying this he left. All the villagers heard what the boy had said. The villagers, privy to the boy's sacrifice, condemned the girl's parents for their unjust treatment of him. As a result, no suitors came forward to marry the girl, despite her affluent background. Eventually, her parents relented and arranged for her to marry a wealthy but unattractive suitor. Displeased with the match, the girl told her friends, "He is so ugly, I don't like him, but since my parents are forcing me to get married to him, I have no other choice but to accept his proposal". This was heard by the boy and he got very angry. He went to her parents and said, *"Uncle (okü), I'm not fit to marry your daughter since I'm ugly and short. I am sorry, I can't marry her"*. His words served as a poignant reminder of the consequences of their actions, leaving them to ponder the true value of wealth and beauty in matters of the heart. Even though she was beautiful and belonged to a rich family, no boys from the village came forward to marry her. Therefore, she remained a spinster till she died.

## NARRATIVE 20: TWO LOVERS OF THE SAME CLAN[31]

Once upon a time there were two people very much in love, a boy and a girl, who longed to marry and build a life together. However, their love was hindered by the fact that they belonged to the same clan, which made their union impossible according to the laws and traditions of their village. Their love was compared to the river *Rüsüayong*, in which the boundaries between the limbs blur and fade. Just as the water of the river flows seamlessly, their love grew deeper and stronger, but they came up against equally strong social rules that prevented them from

[31] Imolemba Jamir (male, 57 years old, Ungma village), oral narration, December 19, 2007.

being together. In a moment of deep regret, they sang a heartbreaking song together, expressing their sorrow and resignation to their fate: "*Kidongzüla lira ipa mezamirarma, kajo mira mira meli küsa teri tongtanger, esabo kodanga melembor*" ("We belong to the same clan, so we can never marry").

## NARRATIVE 21: THE MAN WHO MARRIED HIS COUSIN[32]

Long ago, in a village, there lived a man named *Mangmesoba* who made the controversial decision to marry his paternal cousin against the advice of his parents and other respected elders. After the marriage, *Mangmesoba* planted a sweet potato (yam) in his field and noticed that it was spinning around the support stake in an unnatural, counterclockwise manner. This strange occurrence was a revelation for *Mangmesoba*, leading him to realise the unnaturalness of his union with his cousin sister. He then made the difficult decision to divorce her. The sweet potato that grew in his field became known as *Mangmeso*, symbolising the unconventional nature of his marriage.

## NARRATIVE 22: THE DAUGHTER WHO REFUSED TO MARRY[33]

Once upon a time there was a mother who wanted her daughter to get married as soon as possible, but the daughter never listened to her mother. The daughter always said, "*I am not getting married, I am not*

---

[32] Imolemba Jamir (male, 57 years old, Ungma village), oral narration, December 19, 2007.

[33] Longrichila Longchar (female, 78 years old, Longkhum village), oral narration, December 20, 2007.

*getting married*"34. Marriage was the only way to start a family, because those who do not marry are despised by society. So the mother tried to convince her daughter. She was very disappointed with her daughter's behaviour. One day, the daughter was lying on her mother's lap. The mother took a feather and twisted it back and forth in her daughter's ear. The daughter found the sensation so pleasant and said to her mother, "*Wow! Mother, that's so good, that's so good, do that again*". To which the mother replied, "*That's why I'm telling you to get married if you want to feel this good*". It was only then that the daughter realised her mistake and decided to get married.

## NARRATIVE 23: THE WIFE WHO HELD A COMPETITION WITH HER HUSBAND[35]

Once upon a time there was a happily married couple who divorced due to a simple misunderstanding. After their separation, they lived in separate houses. The husband had a routine of going to the fields every morning with the villagers and returning in the evening to lead a typical life. The wife, on the other hand, tried to challenge her husband by going to the fields alone at dawn, carrying a burning bamboo torch and only returning when the others had long since retired. This behaviour continued for a few days after the divorce. One fateful morning, as she was leaving for the fields, a voice spoke to her and warned her: "*Alu ponga temsenla pesüno nü tali metepla, nabo nuzingabopo matoksatsüji*" ("If you leave early and return late from the fields, you will only get more mosquito bites and you will never surpass your husband"). To her astonishment, the voice belonged to none other than God, who issued a stern warning. This revelation caused her to realise the folly of her actions and to stop competing

---

[34] In the past, it was considered important and breathtaking to get married, both for boys and girls, as there was no education system like the one we have today.
[35] Longrichila Longchar (female, 78 years old, Longkhum village), oral narration, December 20, 2007.

with her ex-husband. From then on, she decided to join forces with the other villagers on their daily outings.


## NARRATIVE 24: STEPMOTHER[36]


Once upon a time in a family, a woman died, leaving behind her husband and son. The husband remarried. The new wife then gave birth to a son. She nourished her son with warm and good food and gave him good clothes and a beautiful cloth woven from the best yarn. Her stepson, on the other hand, she fed with cold and spoilt food and gave him a thick and coarsely woven cotton shawl to wear. The villagers sensed the different treatment the stepmother gave her stepson. One day, the woman asked some villagers, "*Have you seen two boys, one wearing shawl made of soft yarn and the other of coarse yarn?*". They replied, "*We don't see any difference in their shawls*". The mother did not understand why the villagers could not tell the difference between their shawls. One day, while the father and his son were working in the field, they heard the sound of the osü bird. The boy sang to the bird: "*Even if you scream loudly, your meat has a sour taste and your gut is bitter*". The father was shocked when he heard this and said to him, "*Son, why are you singing like that?*". The son replied, "*But father, what can I say, it only tastes like that*". Then the father realised that something was wrong at home when he was not there. So he said to his son, "*Son, tonight I am going to take an osü bird home with me too. I will try some meat from your plate*". The son said, "*It's a pleasure, father*". Then they went back to their house after work. During dinner that night, the husband tasted the food that the wife had served her stepson. He found that she had served him sour leaves and bitter seeds, but not the meat. The father became angry with his wife for treating her stepson badly and expelled his wife and her son from the house that very evening. From then on, the father and son lived alone.


[36] Imolemba Jamir (male, 57 years old, Ungma village), oral narration, December 19, 2007.

## NARRATIVE 25: *SUNGROCHETLA* WHO BECAME A CUCKOO BIRD[37]

In the past, humans, animals and gods lived together. At that time, *Sungrochetla*, the daughter of the god, married a human. She was very pretty and beautiful because her parents fed her with human flesh. One day, *Sungrochetla* said to her husband, "*These days I feel very weak and seem to be losing weight. Can you please go to my parents' house and bring the usual food I used to eat at home?*". He agreed and went to the jungle to meet her parents. He was asked to spend the night with them. The next morning, *Sungrochetla's* parents cut off a human hand, wrapped the hand several times with a leaf called Am and tied it with a bamboo string and gave it to their son-in-law. On the way home, he wanted to see what was inside the leaf, so he slowly opened one of the layers. Each time he tried to open the leaf, a bird (sent by her parents to guide the meal) called out to him: "*Ni nü nangla sayiko*" (I will tell them). When he arrived home, he saw that he had opened all but one layer of the food. He gave the food to his wife, who was making rice beer. She got so excited to receive the food. Afterwards she said to him, "*I'm going to make rice beer now, so go and fetch water or collect firewood in the jungle*". She did this because she didn't want to tell her husband about the food. But he did not trust his wife and peeked through the wall of bamboo mats. He was shocked when he saw her take out a human hand. Then she roasted her hand on the fire and slowly savoured the hand with rice beer. Then her face slowly began to glow and became as beautiful as before.

He told the whole story to his father and asked him for an answer. His father told him: "*You take her to the deep jungle and leave her there*". But the son replied, "*I have a son to take care of, so please do not let me do this business*". So, his father took *Sungrochetla* into the jungle and said to her, "*Let's go and collect yarang (young bananas) in the jungle*". She happily agreed and went into the jungle together. On the way, the

[37] Otsufuba Longkumer (male, 73 years old, Longkhum village), oral narration, December 18, 2007.

father-in-law collected a few clouds and put them in a container. He asked her, "*Do you know this jungle?*". She replied, "*Yes, this is the place we often come to*". The father-in-law thought to himself, "*If I leave her here, she will surely come home, so let me take her to another place*". They walked deeper and deeper into the forest. Finally, they reached a place near a river from which she could not return. Then the father-in-law opened the container of clouds and poured them over her. As a result, the entire neighbourhood was densely covered with clouds so that they could no longer see each other. Then her father told her to wait there for some time until he came back with some leaves. So, he left her in the forest.

*Sungrochetla's* son cried all night looking for his mother's milk, so in the morning her husband said to his father, "*Please go and bring her back, because the baby has been crying all night looking for her*". The father-in-law agreed and went into the forest to look for her. He took food with him. He called out, "*Sungrochetla, Sungrochetla, where are you? I have come to take you home*". But she told him that she had turned half into a human and half into a bird and therefore could not come out. She shouted at him, "*Akongtongdong, akunur ashi kulaker!*" ("Father-in-law is cunning!"). So, he left her half of his food and returned home. He said to his son, "*She will never come back, she has gone to her parents, so take care of your son*".

## NARRATIVE 26: THE SPOILED SON[38]

A long time ago there was a family. They had only one son. He grew up according to his wishes and his parents provided him with all the good food such as fish and meat. To test and see the son's reactions, one evening his parents gave him only a simple dish without meat or fish. The son said to his father, "*Opa nibo ayimnur*" ("Father, I want to scream"). He was trying to say that he wanted some meat or fish. His

[38] Otsufuba Longkumer (male, 73 years old, Longkhum village), oral narration, December 18, 2007.

father quickly replied, "*Tongshi nungji wor ayimang*" ("Go and shout near the wooden post"). Only then did the son realise what his father was trying to say and asked for nothing more. He stopped crossing the line and tried to be a good son.

## NARRATIVE 27: A GIRL WHO TURNS INTO A BIRD[39]

Once upon a time there was a family that had two girls. One day, when their parents were out in the fields, they spent the day collecting firewood. As they went to collect firewood several times, they felt very tired and hungry. The youngest sister asked her older sister, "*Sister, should we get something to eat?*". Her sister replied, "*If you want something to eat, you have to go and collect water first*". When the younger sister asked for food again after returning from the pond, her sister said, "*There are some grains, so you crush the grains*". Finally, she fainted and could no longer do any work due to hunger. She said to her sister, "*I will not do any work because I am very hungry*" and rested. But her sister demanded again, "*You cook the rice first,*" so she started to cook. She took out some rice with a spoon and tasted it to know whether it was cooked or not because she was very hungry. Unfortunately, this action was seen by her older sister. Her sister snatched the spoon from her and beat her terribly. The beating made the younger sister very angry, and she cried hysterically as if she was about to faint. Out of sheer rage, she tore her clothe and put it on her arms and spine so that it looked like the wings and feathers of a bird. When she had arranged it this way, she went to the *sünglang* (balcony) and sang this song: "*Ati mangla süngpeni wangte, Tzüteri mangla, ongpang mentitila nung onglak onglak*" ("Sister, you told me to collect firewood and fetch water, what kind of sister are you?"). When the parents returned from the field, they could not find their youngest daughter. As the sun was about to set, they found her in the corner of the *sünglang*, transformed into a

[39] Otsufuba Longkumer (male, 73 years old, Longkhum village), oral narration, December 18, 2007

bird. She hopped happily and sang the same song she had sung to her older sister. When they saw her and heard the song, they called her many times, thinking that her elder sister might have scolded her and made her very angry. They asked her, "*Child, please come to us. We will scold your sister*". But she never came back to her. The parents scolded the eldest sister, whereupon she also became very angry and never came back to them either. She went down to the balcony, where she also turned into a bird and flew away singing: "*Tenü-a tenü-a!*" ("Sister-o sister!") ("Sister-o sister!"). During the *metsü mapang* (sowing season) you can hear the sound of this bird.

## NARRATIVE 28: TWO BROTHERS AND A TIGER[40]

Once upon a time there were two brothers. They went bird hunting (*anung asai*). They caught many birds, so the younger brother said to his brother, "*Odi (brother), let us go home, we have caught enough birds*". But his brother said to him, "*Let's wait and catch more birds and also catch a big bird for our mother, because when evening comes, many birds will come*". While they were engrossed in their hunt, it became dark. On their way home, they saw an old man walking through the forest with a bamboo torch making a "*mmmh mmmh*" sound. As it was dark and they had no torch with them, they shouted "*Ohhoi! We don't know who you are but wait for me and my brother*". So, the old man was waiting for them. In reality, it was an old tiger. The tiger said to them, "*Burn all the birds, one by one, and put them in my mouth or I will kill you both*". They replied to him, "*We will burn all the birds and give them to you one by one*". Meanwhile, the younger brother said to his brother, "*Brother, do not give the tiger the biggest bird we have caught for our mother*"; he repeated this several times. He took a long stick from the tin, put it on the fire and said to the tiger, "*Grandfather, close your eyes and open your mouth wide, I will give you the biggest bird*". As he did so, the younger brother

---

[40] Tsükdinungba Longkumer (male, 75 years old, Changtongya village), oral narration, April 24, 2008.

put the hot, burning stick in his mouth. His tongue burned and he ran away in search of water. Then they shouted, "*Our enemy is looking for water. Please do not let there be any water in the river!*". When the tiger reached the river, all the water had dried up and he had a hard time with his burnt tongue. This tale wants to say that people get into danger when they live in poor conditions.

## NARRATIVE 29: THE ORIGIN OF TATTOOING[41]

Once upon a time there was an Ao woman, Yarla from *Koridang*, an Ao-Naga settlement. One day, when all the villagers went to the fields, Yarla tied up her younger sister and tattooed her on the leg. It took some time for the wound caused by the tattoo to heal. But the tattoos were much admired by the people after the wounds were completely healed. So, tattooing has been widely used and admired since that time.

## NARRATIVE 30: THE DESIGNS OF TATTOOS[42]

In the past, young girls slept in the *tsüki* (dormitory) at night. Girls from rich and poor families met and spent their time singing and telling stories. There were two girls in the group. One belonged to a rich family from the Chungli clan and the other to a poor family from the Mongsen clan, who was intelligent, beautiful and popular with many of the other girls. The rich girl cultivated jealousy of the poor girl and began to dislike her. The rich girl began to make fun of

[41] Mepolila Imchen (female, 73 years old, Longkhum village), oral narration, December 20, 2007.
[42] Longrichila Longchar (female, 78 years old, Longkhum village), oral narration, December 20, 2007.

the poor girl in front of the other girls. Since the Mongsen girl was very beautiful, the rich girl's mother got a criss-cross tattoo on the Mongsen girl and a parallel tattoo on her daughter out of jealousy. But after the wound on the Mongsen girl's leg healed, she was greatly admired. From that day onwards, the villagers started tattooing and the two groups were tattooed with different patterns. The patterns of their tattoos gave them identity and even the boys found the patterns helpful in distinguishing the girls they admired.

## NARRATIVE 31: TWO GIRLS AND THEIR HAIR[43]

Once upon a time in a village there lived two young girls. The first girl came from a poor background but had a striking beauty and a charming personality. She was known throughout the village for her lush, flowing hair. The second girl, on the other hand, came from a wealthy family, but her hair was short, dull and brown in colour. Despite their different circumstances, the two girls had a close friendship. However, jealousy of her less fortunate companion began to smoulder in the wealthy girl's heart, as she had numerous suitors. As both girls' parents were farmers, they went to the fields together and returned home side by side. Over time, the rich girl began to emphasise her looks. She arrived at the fields on time and was busy styling her hair in various ways in a futile attempt to make it more beautiful. One day, when the villagers had all left for the fields, the poor girl waited patiently for her tardy friend. When she grew tired of the constant delays, she finally plucked up the courage to confront her companion with a song and complained, "*While you fiddle with your hair, those with buns can go, those without must stay*". With that, she set off alone to the fields, leaving her rich friend behind. According to the tale, the poor girl later married and led a wonderful life thanks

---

[43] Otsufuba Longkumer (male, 73 years old, Longkhum village), oral narration, December 18, 2007.

to her hard work. The forefathers say that we cannot change what we
have been given, even if we want to.


## NARRATIVE 32: THE TREE SPIRIT WHO LOVED A GIRL[44]


Once upon a time there was a boy who was in love with a girl from the
Jamir clan. Every night the boy visited her in the girls' dormitory. The
boy only visited her at night. He was very handsome and blessed with
a beautiful singing voice. Every night they spent their time singing
and slept together in the dormitory. When morning came, he got up
early and went back to his place. This happened every day. The girl
became curious about his family and the place where he lived. But
she never had the chance to find out, because he always left early in
the morning when everyone was still asleep and only came back at
night to visit her. One day, the boy asked her to make a *dao* holder
string so that he could wear his *dao* at the *Moatsü* festival (a harvest
festival celebrated in the month of May). As requested, she made a
beautiful *dao* holder for him. The next day, when the girl was on her
way to fetch water, she saw the *dao* holder string she had made tied
to a tree. She untied it and took it back to her dormitory. When the
boy visited the girl that evening, he asked her, "*Why did you take the
cord away from me, I was celebrating the festival*". But the girl did not
believe him and told him, "*Don't lie to me! I took it away because I saw
it tied to a tree near the pond*". They then ended their conversation and
spent their time singing. When the boy got up early in the morning,
the girl decided to follow him secretly. She saw his image all the way
to the end of the village, but just after she crossed the village, she saw
him turn into a tree (*amtong*). She saw the tree go down and stopped
near the pond from which she had fetched water the previous day.
When she went closer to look at the tree, she realised that it was the

---

[44] Otsufuba Longkumer (male, 73 years old, Longkhum village), oral narration,
December 18, 2007.

same tree she had encountered yesterday. Only then did she realise that she was in love with a tree spirit. She built herself a bed out of this tree. When she slept on the bed, she died because the spirit of the tree took her away because it was her lover. In the past and even today, Jamir women are not allowed to sleep or sit on anything made from this tree because it is believed that they will die very soon, and their lives are in danger.

## NARRATIVE 33: THE BOY WHO CHOSE HIS WIFE[45]

Once upon a time there was a young boy. He wanted to get married but could not find the perfect match for himself. As time passed in his search for a wife, he chose two girls from his village. To choose the best of the two, he decided to take the girls fishing. He wanted to observe their character, personality and manners and study whether they were lazy, hardworking or cunning. He picked a nice day and took the two girls fishing. They caught a lot of fish and cooked for themselves. During lunch, the first girl said to the boy, *"I'm very excited today because we have caught lots of fish. We are so lucky. I am enjoying this fish"*. But the second girl told him with a smile, *"I'm not hungry, so do not let me eat anything, not even the fish. When the boy heard that, he said to her, "Why don't you just take the fish?"* So, she touched the cooked fish lightly with her finger, put the touched finger on her tongue and said, *"Yes, it's very tasty, really tasty"*. She was attempting to demonstrate that she had a light appetite. Observing her behaviour, the boy inferred that something was amiss. After finishing their lunch, they returned to the village. Instead of heading home, the boy went directly to the second girl's house and discreetly observed through the wall. To his astonishment, he witnessed the girl preparing and eating yum (*manü*). Having gone without food the

[45] Imolemba Jamir (male, 57 years old, Ungma village), oral narration, December 19, 2007. A different version of this tale can be found in Mills work *The Ao Nagas* (1926), titled as "The Story of Aviachukla" (321-22).

entire day, she expressed her hunger to her mother by saying, "*Avi achet rok, avi achet rok*" ("Mother peel off the skin, mother peel off the skin"). Out of hunger, she enlisted her mother's help to quickly peel the skin off the yum. Each time the girl consumed a piece of yum, the boy placed a small stone on his shawl, amassing a collection of stones. Subsequently, the boy returned to his own home. That evening, the young man gathered the stones he had collected and made his way to the girls' dormitory. Upon arriving, he presented the stones to the girls and posed a question, "*If these stones were cooked to perfection, do you believe a person could consume this much?*" The first girl responded enthusiastically, claiming she could easily consume double the number of stones presented. She even mentioned having eaten more food after returning from a fishing trip. However, the second girl expressed doubt, stating that it would be impossible for a person to eat such a large quantity. Without hesitation, the young man confronted the second girl, revealing that he had witnessed her consuming a similar amount of food earlier that evening. The girl was left feeling embarrassed by the revelation. Ultimately, the young man chose the first girl as his ideal partner.[46]

---

[46] In another version of the story, the boy's mother tested the girls by asking them to come and collect flowers from her house. In the past, girls were very fond of flowers. The girls used different kinds of flowers to decorate themselves. The boy's mother collected some flowers knowing the fact that the girls will love to have it. She placed the flowers on the *sapang* (backside kind of balcony). Before they come, she scattered the dishes and plates all over the house and near the doors. The mother called the girls to the house and told them, "*I have collected and kept some flowers on the sapang so if you want to decorate your ears with those flowers then go and get it from the sapang*". Having said the word flower, the *Mongsen* girl went straight to get the flowers without noticing the dishes and the plates on the floors, but the *Chungli* girl cautiously picked up the things lying on the floor, placed them properly as she went to get the flowers. After she had placed the things properly, only then she went to get the flowers. Looking at the different manners and behaviour of the girls, the mother came to know that her son's choice was perfect.

## NARRATIVE 34: THE EMBARRASSING BOY[47]

Once upon a time, there was a boy who belonged to the *Mongsen* clan. He was in love with a *Chungli* girl and wanted to marry her. To win her heart, he began to visit the girl's dormitory. Society expects a boy to be hard-working and to know all types of work before he looks to get married. Keeping all of this in mind, the boy used to work hard to win the girl's heart. He used to visit the girl's house and help her family in their work. One day, as the boy was having food with the girl's family, the boy sat next to the girl's father. When the boy was trying to tear off a piece of meat from his food with his teeth, the meat slipped and fell onto the father's plate. Noticing the fallen piece of meat on his plate, the father asked him: *"You don't want to have this meat?"*. Since he did not want to embarrass himself, the boy quickly answered, *"Yes, yes uncle!"*. After they had finished their food, the boy went to fetch water for them. After he collected the water on the bamboo, he tied the bamboo with a rope, but he didn't know that he had tied the bamboo along with the roots on the ground. He tried to pull the basket, but he could not do it. At last, when he tried to pull the basket filled with water on the bamboos, the force broke the rope attached to the root, and water dropped on the ground. Unfortunately, when the bamboos dropped to the ground, he fell onto some chicks that belonged to the girl's family and killed some of them. Considering the behaviour of the boy, the girl's father thought to himself that something was wrong with the boy and decided not to let his daughter marry him. When the boy came to her house, the father told him, *"From today onward stop visiting our house and go to some other house"*. With this, the father meant to say that he rejected the boy becoming his son-in-law.

[47] Imolemba Jamir (male, 57 years old, Ungma village), oral narration, December 19, 2007.

# NARRATIVE 35: THE IMPROPER MARRIAGE[48]

Once upon a time, in the villages of Changtongya and Akhoya, a love story unfolded that captured the attention of all who heard it. A young man named Imsükumba from Akhoya found himself in love with a young woman named Songopo Longkumer from Changtongya, and he knew he wanted to make her his wife. The news of their love quickly spread throughout both villages, causing a stir among the residents. Imsükumba approached his parents to seek their blessing for the union, only to be met with a surprising response. His parents insisted that his elder brother must marry Songopo first, as he was still unmarried. Despite his disappointment, Imsükumba respected his parents' wishes and remained silent, unable to go against their decision. In a selfless act of sacrifice, Imsükumba and Songopo agreed to let his brother marry her instead. Although Songopo did not love her new husband, she tried her best to adjust to her new life and make the marriage work. However, the strain of the situation proved too much for both of them, and their unhappiness only grew. Tragically, Songopo's heart could not bear the weight of her unfulfilled love, and she passed away soon after. The once-happy family was left shattered and broken, with no one finding true happiness in the end.[49]

[48] Imolemba Jamir (male, 57 years old, Ungma village), oral narration, December 19, 2007.

[49] According to the narrator, this tale serves as a poignant reminder of the power of love and the consequences of sacrificing one's own happiness for the sake of others. It is a cautionary tale of the importance of following one's heart and not letting societal expectations dictate one's fate.

## NARRATIVE 36: THE SON WHO WENT TO THE LAND OF THE DEAD[50]

Once upon a time, a family consisting of two sons tragically lost their parents, leaving them to fend for themselves. The brothers worked tirelessly in the fields each day, only to find their work mysteriously completed by the next morning. Intrigued by this phenomenon, the elder brother, Imolemba, suggested they stay overnight to uncover the source of this assistance. As they quietly observed from their field hut that night, they were astonished to see the spirits of their deceased parents toiling away. In a sudden move, the brothers attempted to capture their parents, but the father managed to escape. Moved by pity, the mother whisked the younger son away to the mystical land of death, *Asü yim*. In *Asü yim*, the son found himself surrounded by unseen voices and was instructed by his mother to join the people on a wild boar hunt. Armed with a spear, he followed the voices, only to come face to face with a grasshopper, *songkok*. In a moment of confusion, he instinctively struck the grasshopper with his spear, triggering a chorus of voices proclaiming his action, "*Akumliba-i songkok tsüngoko*" (The one who has life killed the grasshopper). The mother waited for her son to come home. When he returned from the hunt, his mother said to him, "*Son, our world and your world are different, so please go back to your brother. Even though I love you and don't want to let you go, we have to leave*". Realising the vast difference between their worlds, the mother tearfully bid her son farewell, urging him to return to his brother. She packed provisions for his journey and cautioned him not to open them until he reached his destination. She warned him, "*Do not open this parcel before you cross the Longridong River. Go straight to your brother*". Nevertheless, he was very curious to see what was inside and opened the parcel before crossing the river. To his horror, he found only ashes and pig faeces. He continues his journey. After crossing the river, he decided to open the parcel again. This time he found the parcel filled

---

[50] Imolemba Jamir (male, 57 years old, Ungma village), oral narration, December 19, 2007.

with rice and meat. After meeting his brother, they shared the food. After separating from his mother, he continued to live on earth with his brother as a normal human being.

## NARRATIVE 37: LIJABA AND THE TWO GIRLS[51]

One day, *Lijaba*, the creator of the earth, decided to embark on a journey to explore different parts of the world. After traveling for many days, he arrived at a village one evening. Seeking shelter for the night, *Lijaba* went from door to door, only to be turned away by every family in the village, each offering a different excuse. However, at the end of the village, *Lijaba* came across a small house where two sisters resided. Despite their poverty, the sisters welcomed *Lijaba* with open arms when he asked for shelter. They expressed their inability to cook due to their lack of food, but *Lijaba* instructed them to warm water in a pot. To their amazement, a grain of rice emerged from his knee and filled the pot when placed inside. Subsequently, a piece of meat appeared from his forehead, which they cooked and enjoyed together. After dinner, *Lijaba* and the sisters stood outside the house, where he inquired about the neighbouring fields. Learning that the fields belonged to the families who had rejected the sisters, *Lijaba* proceeded to curse the fields, wishing for them to yield only tusks. Upon discovering the sisters' own small rice field, they hesitated to reveal its ownership out of shame. However, *Lijaba* encouraged them to share the truth, and upon learning that it belonged to them, he blessed the field, declaring it would yield non-stop harvests. In this tale, *Lijaba's* actions serve as a reminder of the importance of kindness and humility, as well as the power of blessings and curses.

[51] Otsufuba Longkumer (male, 73 years old, Longkhum village), oral narration, December 18, 2007.

## NARRATIVE 38: LIJABA'S SPIRIT[52]

In the old days, people worshipped *Lijaba* as the creator of the earth. But no one has seen him. The *arasentsür* (witch doctor or magician) was the only intermediary between the people and Lijaba. One day, Lijaba said to the *arasentsür*, "*I will no longer live on this earth among the people. Instead, I will send my spirit to bless or punish them, depending on what good or evil they have done. People will know when I am coming. Therefore, everyone should celebrate a feast to commemorate my name. One should sacrifice a perfect, healthy and complete animal without any disability or scar on the body. The flesh of the animal should not be shared with anyone. Even the bone should not be broken*". So, one summer a grasshopper appeared. People thought it was the spirit of *Lijaba* and shouted, 'Lijaba's *sungkok* (Lijaba's locust) has come'. It only stayed for two to three weeks and then disappeared. When the people saw the locust, they announced to each other that *Lijaba's* spirit had come to earth. The entire village revered and sought blessings from him. The Ao people believe that the grasshopper embodies the spirit of *Lijaba*, and therefore, they venerate it as a symbol of the god *Lijaba*.

## NARRATIVE 39: MOON COVERED WITH COW DUNG[53]

Long ago, it was believed that the moon was closer to the earth than the sun, resulting in it being warmer than the sun and causing excessive heat for human beings. The people of the earth found it unbearable to endure the intense heat from the moon's rays and sought help from *Aningtsüngba*, the god of heaven who had the power to control the movements of the sun and moon. Upon hearing their pleas,

[52] Otsufuba Longkumer (male, 73 years old, Longkhum village), oral narration, December 18, 2007.
[53] Otsufuba Longkumer (male, 73 years old, Longkhum village), oral narration, December 18, 2007.

*Aningtsüngba* acted by throwing cow dung on the face of the moon to reduce its heat and brightness during the nights. This act caused the moon to feel ashamed and prompted it to slowly move away from the earth and the sun. To this day, this tale is passed down by the elders as a reminder of the power of the gods and the importance of seeking their intervention in times of need.

## NARRATIVE 40: THE CURSED MANGO TREE[54]

In the village of Longkhum, there resided a wealthy man. One year, a bountiful harvest of rice was reaped from his fields, bringing great joy to his daughters. They marvelled at their father's success, exclaiming to one another, "*Of all the clans in the village, our father has truly excelled*". Eager to share the news, they instructed the women of their clans and their sisters-in-law to prepare five pots of rice beer each, in order to assist with the task of moving the rice to the storage room over the course of five days. As they made their way to the fields, the women came across a Naga mango tree laden with ripe fruit. Despite their desire to partake, none could reach the mangoes. Frustrated, they vented their frustration by cursing and spitting at the tree, uttering, "*jakrep-a sangni, jakrep-a sangni*" (break and die, beak and die). To their amazement, while working in the fields, they witnessed the mango tree collapse to the ground. Overjoyed, they proclaimed, "*The curse of Longkhum has been answered. We have triumphed!*" Returning to the village after five days, the women shared the tale of their success. It is believed among the villagers that the curses of the Longkhum women hold great power, as evidenced by the fallen mango tree. This serves as a reminder to refrain from unnecessary spitting, as even the mango tree was not spared from their potent words.

---

[54] Longrichila Longchar (female, 78 years old, Longkhum village), oral narration, December 20, 2007.

# 3

# ORIGIN AND DISPERSAL OF NAGAS: A FOLKLORIC PERSPECTIVE

The origins and migration patterns of the Naga people remain shrouded in mystery due to the absence of their own written documentation. Not until the early 1830s did the British Empire begin its military expeditions to secure control over the Naga Hills, eventually leading to a comprehensive ethnographic survey that documented the different tribes through articles and monographs. The British administrators-ethnologists were drawn to the distinctiveness of the Nagas and spent significant time conducting thorough research and documentation on their traditions, beliefs, and way of life. Therefore, the advancement of Naga ethnography coincided with the expansion of the British Empire in the Naga Hills. Colonial Officers, Western Missionaries and Scholars have put forth differing theories in their works regarding the Naga tribes' arrival and settlement in their current habitat. While many hold on the notion that Naga tribes arrived in their present location from diverse directions and in different waves, rather than all at once, it is widely believed that the Nagas originated from multiple Southeast Asian lands. According to certain academics, there is also a belief that they have ties to Mongolians who migrated to the hilly areas. It is worth noting that despite the absence of a written history of their own, their folklore, folktales, and legends serve as valuable sources for understanding their origins.

Over an extended period, numerous researchers have studied the cultural and ethnological attributes of the Nagas through examining their speculated coastal lineage, physical features, language origins, and customary practices. In addition, they draw comparisons between the Nagas and various other tribes in South-East Asia, exploring the potential roots of the Nagas in the Philippines. The following paragraphs studies the varying perspectives of writers on the cultural and ethnological characteristics of the Nagas.

According to Shakespear, Nagas shows similarities with the Dyaks in their counting methods, domestic tools, village architecture, and head-hunting practices. The Dyaks makes extensive use of the saltwater shells which are not found in Naga regions. However, despite residing in remote inland areas, the Nagas preference for marine shells indicates a possible coastal lineage (1914, 197). Mary Maid Clark (1978, 43) described the Nagas as characterised by their medium stature and lighter skin tone in comparison to the indigenous populations of Bengal or Africa. Ethnologically, they are believed to have Indo-Chinese or Tibeto-Burman descent, and their languages demonstrate a high level of cognitive complexity.

The Nagas and the Austro-Asian stock are compared by W.C Smith. He believes that the buffalo's use in the Naga Hills, both as a domestic animal and as a carving emblem, is linked to this Austro-Asian stock, as is the practise of terracing the hillsides and possibly the establishment of permanent settlements in villages with shifting, but not migratory, agriculture (2002, xii). He tries to outline thirteen Naga qualities that are widespread among Indonesians (the people of Malaya and the island of Indonesia). Headhunting, a shared sleeping chamber for unmarried males, and the disposal of the deceased are only a few of them. This demonstrates that the Nagas were once intimately associated with South-East Asian tribes, particularly the Dyaks of Borneo, the Battacks of Sumatra, the Igords, and other Philippians and Formosan tribes.

According to M. Horam, the current group of Nagas originated in the Philippines. His argument is based on the fact that the Philippines has a village named 'Naga' (1975, 25). The aforementioned belief, however, is simply an assumption because the Naga village (now Naga city) in the Philippines was originally named by Spanish forces in 1573 after they discovered a flourishing Bikol village with an abundance of narra trees in the area. Because they were left undisturbed for such a long period, the Naga have preserved their old civilisation to this day. Their use of Cowries shells as ornaments (precious ornaments for them), as well as the fact that the Nagas have many customs and ways of life that are very similar to those of those living in remote parts of Borneo, Sarawak, Indonesia, Malaysia, and elsewhere, suggests that their ancient abode was near the sea, if not in some islands (Shimray, 1985, 13).

Conch shells and cowries are used by the Nagas to decorate their clothing. Butler was told by the people of Rengma (Tesopheneyee) in 1874, as the leader of an exploring expedition party, that they had dominated "The Coast for Ages" (Bareh, H., 1970, 19). This indicates that the forefathers may have traveled along a shoreline. Long drums hewn from massive wood also incorporate canoes, which are very popular among islanders. Panger Imchen even compares the Nagas' method of slaying Mithun to that of the Vietnamese. In both cases, the dao technology and the process of drinking beer during celebratory occasions are similar (Imchen, 1990).

## ORIGIN MYTHS ABOUT NAGA MIGRATION

The Naga migrations are mentioned in the oral tradition, particularly in myths. The sacred narratives that recount how the world came into being are known as myths. The stories describe how the Supreme Being discloses his mysteries through creation, the human and animal kingdom's place in the universe, and their interaction, among other things. According to Marca Eliade, myth is a factual and sacred history that tells the account of an event that occurred in primaeval time, the mythical time of the origins. Myths describe how a reality, whether the entire reality, the cosmos, or just a portion of reality, came into being because of the actions of Supreme Beings. Myth is always an account of creation. It relates how something was produced, began to be. The myth tells only what had really happened and which manifested it completely (1963, 1).

According to oral traditions, the Nagas originated in mainland China and came to Myanmar by rivers and passageways. For generations, they journeyed to the southern seas of Myanmar by river and settled along the shores of Moulmein. Eventually, they relocated to the valleys of the Irrawaddy and Chindwin rivers. They resided in the Irrawaddy valley for generations but were most likely driven away by more advanced races in conflict. The Nagas migrated from the Irrawaddy Valley to Manipur via the Indo-Myanmar corridor, where they eventually arrived at the Makhel (the spot where the Nagas dispersed), a historical landmark in Senapati, Manipur District. Many Nagas are thought to have diverged from Makhel and migrated to the current Naga inhabited territories. The origin myth of the Nagas, namely Narrative 1: 'Tiger, Spirit, and Man' explores the connection between the settlement of Makhel and the Mao-Nagas, detailing their origins and migration. This myth sheds light on the intricate history and cultural heritage of the Nagas, highlighting the interwoven relationships between different tribes within the region.[55]

According to myth, Nagas lived in a mythical realm where terrestrial beings (humans and animals) and celestial beings (sky, clouds, and spirits) coexisted in the same environment for sustenance and continuity. Humans eventually learned to survive by employing the bow and arrow to hunt other living species (hunting). People began to separate from their fellow beings as they began to acquire land for shifting cultivation. As a result, the animals went into the forests and the spirits vanished into the skies leaving the lands to humans. The myth depicts an unexpected union between the woman (earth) and the clouds (symbolising solidified waters, and indeed semen) that resulted in the birth of three atypical uterine siblings–Man, Tiger, and Spirit, who indeed shared the same habitat. To this day, the Nagas believe that some people have the soul of a tiger. It is said that when a person

---

[55] For further readings refer: Lorho Mary Maheo, *The Mao Naga tribe of Manipur: a Demographic Anthropological Study*, New Delhi, Mittal Publications, 2004, pp. 21-22

with such a soul dies, a tiger in the forest dies as well. If the tiger is injured, the person who has the tiger soul is hurt as well. Similarly, it is believed that spirits that damage or threaten humans by their miracles will hide among large trees, unused water ponds in the forest, deserted spots, and so forth. Other Naga communities have similar myths with various changes (Interview with Tsükdinungba Longkumer (M), 75 years old, Changtongya village, 24 April 2008; Imolemba Jamir (M), 57 years, Ungma village, 19 December 2007).

The Nagas, like any other animists, trace their origins to animate and inanimate things of the world like trees and stones. The above-explained origin myth got actualised symbolically in the form of a Banyan tree (*Marabu*), (Nepuni 2010: 38) stones of Man, Tiger, and Spirit at Makhel in Manipur district. They still stand as cultural icons of Naga identity for the people remember the myth whenever they see them. Indeed, many Nagas still commit the myth to memory. The following panel of photographs shows the sites to which origin myths are associated.

Photo 3.1: Panel of photographs. The Sacred tree in Makhel (1), the stones of Man (2), Spirit (3), and Tiger (4).[56]

Narrative 1 recounts the journey of the Nagas from their ancestral homeland of Makhel in Manipur to Khezhakeno in Chakhesang and eventually to various parts of the northeast region. This narrative also explains the origins of the Angamis, Sumis, Lothas, and Rengmas, four prominent Naga tribes. The Angami-Naga rendition of this origin myth (Narrative 2) sheds light on the migration patterns of these tribes. Of course, the history of how the Naga tribes came to occupy their current position had vanished into the dim obscurity of folklore

[56]https://www.facebook.com/media/set/?set=a.233868789978619.66506.227200567312108&type=1.Accessed: 30 Nov, 2011.

(Hutton, 1921). The Angami-Nagas are believed to be descended from two forefathers who emerged from the depths of the earth, not in Angami territory, but likely in Manipur or a southern region. By examining into this myth, we can gain a deeper understanding of the migration origins of the Naga tribes. This narrative provides valuable insights into the cultural and historical roots of these communities, offering a glimpse into their rich and complex heritage.

In Khezhakeno village the 'supposed origin stone' is being still preserved (Ghosh, 1979, 39). The Angami myth (Narrative 2) illustrates the journey of the Nagas and their subsequent division into different clans. The aforementioned folk narrative motif is common in Nagaland, where other sects relate a similar tale about their origins and migration. The Ao-Nagas Longchar clan claims to have descended from the same stone slab in Khezhakeno where grain was strewn for thrashing. Even yet, the Nagas regard this origin tale

**Photo 3.2:** This stone or monolith is kept in memory as Naga dispersal Site, Khezhakeno.[57]

and its connection to the stone slab with respect and reverence. The following photograph shows the mythical stone slab at Khezhakeno:

## MYTHICAL LORE ON AO-NAGA ORIGIN AND MIGRATION

The Ao-Naga as one of the many tribes with origin myths are distinct from those of their sister-tribes. They are still very passionate about their origins and the symbolism associated with them. Those who violate their culture by distorting it are usually fined in cash or kind (Mills, 1926, 5). During an interview in 2005, Chubameren Longchar (76 years), a community culture specialist, is afraid to discuss the origin myths of the other clans who live in his village, even though he knows them. He seeks to protect himself from unwelcome disputes that put him in harm's way. Seeking safety, he aims to prevent himself from getting caught up in unwanted disputes that could jeopardise his well-being. As a result, the Ao-Naga tribe's identity and origin myths are meticulously developed and legally safeguarded. Because the Ao tribe is made up of several villages and sub-clans, each has its own set of rules and regulations.

In the same manner that Naga is a given name for the tribe, it is believed that 'Ao' is a name given by Sangtam, Chang, Phom, and Konyak Nagas to a group of people who deviated from a larger group. The term "Ao" means "went or went away" in the context of people who migrated across the Dikhu River in Mon district to settle among the Aos. This oral tradition is prevalent among the Nagas and serves as evidence of the divergence of the Ao-Nagas from other Naga groups.

According to tradition, after a lengthy time of life at Chungliyimti (now in Tuensang district), the inhabitants were compelled to acquire more land as their population rose exponentially. As a result, groups of individuals headed off for a western location. They had to cross the

---

[57] https://www.facebook.com/photo.php?fbid=233932013305630&set=a.2339313 03305701.66513.227200567312108&type=3&theater. 30 November 2011.

Dikhu River to get to their goal. After that, they built a cane bridge. Aos was the first of the group to reach the other side of the river. They cut off the bridge as soon as they landed on the bank, intending for no one to cross over to their side. Hence, those who crossed the Dikhu River[58] were known as "Aor" or "Ao" meaning "went or went away" and those who were left behind came to be known as "*Merir*" meaning "left out" or "left behind" (interview with Imolemba Jamir, 57 years, Ungma village, 19 December 2007). Till today, the Ao people call the other tribes like Sangtam, Chang, Phom, and Konyak as *Merir*. This is how the word "Ao" and "*Merir*" originated.

The Sumi tribes of Nagaland have a unique way of referring to the different tribes in the region. They call the Aos "Cholimi," which translates to "the people of Chungliyimti" or "gone ahead." The Lothas are referred to as "*Chuwomi*," meaning "who proceeded," and the Angamis are known as "*Tsungumi*," which means "left behind." This interesting naming convention highlights the historical movement of the Aos ahead of the other tribes in the region. However, Panger Imchen challenges the aforementioned assumption regarding the origin of the Ao people and argues that the Aos actually referred to themselves as "Ahors," placing emphasis on the term "Ho," which translates to "mountain" or "mountain dwellers" in various dialects. (Imchen, 1993, 20).

The Aos address the Sumi Naga as "*Moyar*" which means, "not hungry." As B. B. Ghosh states every term or name originates with meaning either through an accident or through a story linked to it (1979, 2), Aos tell the following account concerning the naming of the "*Moyars*" as Sumi Nagas (interview Otsufuba Longkumer (M), 73 years old, Longkhum village, on 18 December, 2007).

Once upon a time, the Aos and the Semas were working together. The Aos inquired if the Sumis were hungry, to which the Sumis replied

---

[58] I. Bendangangashi and I. T. Apok Aier (Naga scholars of the 20th century) feel that the mentioned Dikhu River cannot be the exact river. But for them, "it may be one of the big tributaries of the Irrawadi like the Chinwin River in Myanmar (Burma)", I. Bendangangshi Aier and I. T. Apok Aier, *The Religion of the Ao Nagas*, Guwahati, 1990: X).

that they were not. From that moment on, the Aos began referring to the Sumis as "*moya*," which translates to the not-hungry group.

## AO-NAGAS' WORLDVIEW ON THEIR ORIGINS

The Ao-Naga worldview contains abundant lore about their origin and nomenclature of their clans. Their mythical lore represents the Ao-Naga folklife's emergence with the cosmos of animate and inanimate creations. The origin myths provide information on (i) how the god created the geography and environment of their Ao-Naga land, (ii) how Ao-Naga clans originated from inanimate matter, the stones (*Longterok*-six stones), and (iii) how clans originated from celestial beings, birds, and animals, and their remains such as feathers, as well as celestial bodies such as the sky, clouds, wind, and waters.

## THE GEOGRAPHY AND ENVIRONMENT OF AO-LAND AS REFLECTED IN THE MYTH OF *LIJABA*, THE CREATOR

The Ao-Nagas, like all other Naga tribals, regard the earth and nature as life-giving creatures that cannot be separated from any aspect of their sustenance and endurance. They establish identities and continuities with all of the god's living and non-living creations, with a focus on land and environment. They see land as a substratum for social groups to develop communal as well as personal identities for their members, rather than just space to be optimised for survival. They think that humans, nature, animals, and insects all share common ancestral roots and hence share a personal and communal bond. Animals, like humans, take part in decision-making and have a strong sense of discernment and gratitude. Humans are a part of creation, not something separate from it. The Supreme Being (*tsungrem*) was personified as *Lijaba*, the Creator, who escaped the steep terrains, rivers, streams, ponds, wooded lands, and so on for the Ao-Nagas, according to the following story. There are two *Lijaba* myths about the creation of landscapes and the Aos' sustenance that are generally held in the community. *Tsungrem* is seen as both the creator and the sustainer of human humans on the earth. He builds the universe, guards against evil, and bestows fortunes. The myth of *Lijaba* and his creation (narrative No. 3) explains the mythical causes behind Nagaland's mountainous terrain.

As a result, the myth establishes a geographical contrast between Assam's plains and Nagaland's, with the former having plains and the latter having hills, forest, deep valleys, and other features. It also says that the Assamese are the most likely outside threat to the Ao-Nagas. Mills' version of water cockroach is actually a water beetle (1926, 220). It is necessary to explain the historical grounds for the conflict between the Assamese and the Aos in this section. The Nagas had already established themselves in the southeastern Burmese region when the Ahoms arrived in 1228 under King Sukhapa (Chasie, 257-58) . The Nagas and the Ahoms have a long history of interaction dating back to the 13$^{th}$ century A.D. Disputes between the two groups were frequent, with the Nagas expressing concerns about potential encroachment on their land by the Ahoms. This led to raids by the Nagas on Ahom homes and the looting of their possessions, resulting in ongoing conflict between the two parties. One significant event was the Ahoms' invasion of the Kachari capital, Dimapur, during which they crossed Ao land. However, their attempts to assist the Raja of Manipur in 1765-1767 were hindered by the dense jungles of Naga land. The Ahoms saw multiple opportunities to engage in conflict with the Nagas in pursuit of their political and commercial interests, leading to the establishment of Nagakhats - unique trading markets where Nagas could conduct business and defend against tribal attacks. In an effort to maintain peace and security, the Ahoms even paid the Nagas a form of protection money to prevent raids on those who complied. Despite initial animosity, prolonged warfare, and failed attempts at subjugation, the proximity and economic interdependence between the two groups have fostered a relationship of mutual reliance over time.

These historical connections show that the tumultuous Naga tribe has been in instability for a long time, and that they have had to keep on their toes to protect their kingdoms from neighbouring invaders. The fear reflected in the faulty and disorganised development of Ao kingdoms in Nagaland is reflected in the Supreme Creator, *Lijaba*. Because he is the protector and sustainer of the people, his major task is to protect them from enemies. As a result, to avoid the enemies, he left the location. The myth explains the origin of Ao-geographical land in terms of the political issues that existed at the period.

In the Aos' worldview, the water cockroach is a benefactor. Raw cockroaches are used as medicine by the Aos to treat diseases including tuberculosis and asthma. The scientific name for this species is *Blatta orienta*. Some of the local names are *leplu* (Ao), *balno* (Angami), *plau* (Sumi), *mejingping* (Khiamniungan), *luplyue* (Lotha), *phelew* (Rengma), *akalü* (Pochury), *takapui* (Zeliang), and (Chakhesang) (N. S. Jamir and P. Lal, 2005, 100–104).

The protection of the entire Nagas' humankind from attack and annihilation can be likened to the way cockroaches protect humans from disease. Just as the cockroach drove *Lijaba* to complete his work as the enemy drew near, he finished in a daring manner and proceeded to confront the opponents. The Ao-landscape remains impervious to enemy attacks and inaccessible to invaders due to its topographical limitations. Consequently, *Lijaba* and the cockroach may have the ability to safeguard the people and the environment from foreign invasions. By associating the formation of their landscapes and surroundings with their supreme god *Lijaba*, the Ao-Nagas have legitimised their ownership of their region as a gift from god. In essence, the narrative provides a mythical explanation for the current structure of Ao-land and its environment.

*Lijaba* descends with the seeds into the earth and rises with the crop. *Lijaba* is the one who created and continues to create the earth; he is the one who protects, upholds, sustains, and gives life to all. As a result, the Supreme Being is the exclusive owner of the entire universe. Tribals have a feeling of time and distance because of the activities related with the earth and seasons of the environment. They concentrate their attention on the land since time is cyclical. People believe that the years will pass in an endless cycle, just as the sun rises and sets and the moon waxes and wanes. They wish for events like the rainy season, planting, sowing, harvesting, and dry seasons to linger indefinitely. The concept of time revolves around the celebration of nature's life cycle. Folklife is also disturbed when nature is disrupted. The tribal concept of history and time is entwined with and anchored in creation (A. Wati Longchar, Yangkllhao Vashum 1998, 83–89). As a result, in order to sustain their identity and continuity, the people mythologise and mystify their connection to the land and environment.

## ORIGIN OF THE AO PEOPLE FROM STONES: THE MYTH OF LONGTEROK (SIX STONES)

The Ao-Nagas' prevalent idea about their origin is that their forefathers came from the six stones of *Longterok*. As a result, a sacred narrative about their origins was created under the guise of the *Longterok* myth. *Longterok*, according to Ao myth, is made up of two words: *Long*, which means stone, and *terok*, which means six. As a result, Longterok's literal meaning is 'six stones', (Interview with Otsufuba Longkumer, 73 years, Longkhum village, 18 December 2007). *Longterok*, in Chungliyimti, Tuensang District, was named for the village that sprang up around these six stones. The origin is mythologised, and the myth is articulated through geographic locations and relics. As a result, the Aos created cultural memories in their collective mind. The stories and memory stones that represent the originators both help to keep the Naga society's Ao-Naga origins alive. The stones at Chungliyimti, Tuensang District, are shown in the photo below:

**Photo 3.3**: Remains of *Longterok*

The *Longterok* myth is a captivating tale that is passed down through generations as a rich oral tradition among the Ao-Nagas. The narrative features names that are unique to this particular cultural group, adding to the mystique and authenticity of the story. According to the myth, six individuals emerged from a stone, believed to be the progenitors of the three clans. Each clan is represented by a pair consisting of one male and one female, symbolising the balance and harmony within the community. This myth serves as a powerful reminder of the origins and unity of the Ao people, reinforcing the importance of tradition and heritage in their collective identity. The males and females of three clans are shown in the table below:

| Male and Female | Clan |
|---|---|
| Tongpok (M), Lungkupokla (F) | Pongener |
| Longpok (M), Yongmenyala (F) | Longkumer |
| Longjakrep (M), Elangshi (F) | Jamir |

**Table 3.1:** Clan-wise distribution of humans having emerged from the stones

Tongpok, a Pongen male, married to Elangshi, a Jamir female; Longjakrep, a Jamir male, married to Yongmenyala, a Longkumer female; and Longpok, a Longkumer male, married to Lungkupokla, a Pongen female. Among the Aos, these three clans were the most powerful. As time passed, three additional sub-clans emerged as a result of these (interview Otsufuba Longkumer, 73 years, Longkhum village, 18 December 2007).

The following diagram describes the origination of the Ao tribes.

The Ao Mongsen do not believe in the *Longterok's* narrative of an above-ground origin myth. They claim that Chungliyimti village was their first home. The Chungli Aos of the Ongpangkong range are considered Mongsen Aos' descendants. The Imchen, Longchar, and Walling clans of the Mongsen Aos, on the other hand, claim that they are not sprung from stones or the Chungli group. "The Mongsen came out of the earth first and settled at Kubok, a vacant site on a spur going down from Mokongtsu towards the Dikhu River," according to

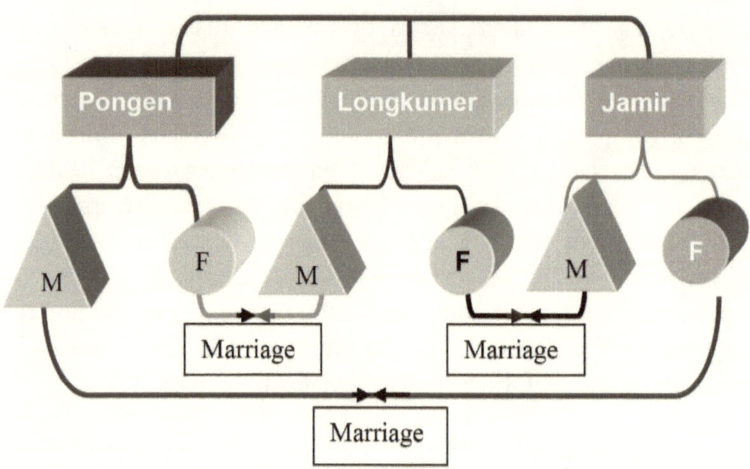


**Diagram 3.1:** Origination of Ao-clans. Ao-Naga origin stones: Longterok


J. P. Mills (1926, 7). However, there is occasional inter-tribal warfare between these two groups, according to folklore. The most well-known example is when the Mongsen Aos used to kill Chungli Aos in such a way that the latter couldn't figure out who was to blame. Shiluti, a legendary Chungli hero, was the only one capable of defeating the Mongsen Aos and resolving the issue. The Mongsen Aos were eventually obliged to come to Chungliyimti village and establish a *khel* alongside the Chungli.

Ever since the inception of the Ao-Naga society, the *Chungli* Aos and *Mongsen Aos*, never had any common administration unit even if they lived together in a common village and the same practice is retained till today. This account is embedded in the narrative 'The attack on Kubok village', which narrates the story of a young man named Shiluti who discovers a blocked path while hunting. He clears the path and follows it to a settlement where headless bodies were found. Shiluti informs his wife, but the information is overheard by locals who inform the village elders. The elders invite Shiluti to a meeting where they plan to attack the Kubok settlements. Shiluti is tasked with training and evaluating the village warriors. He conducts a ritual involving a pig and successfully trains the warriors. The Mongsen

Aos are defeated when they attack the Kubok village, leading to the construction of a *khel* in Chungliyimti and the alliance between the Chungli Aos and the Mongsen Aos.

Although the Mongsen Aos do not claim descent from the *Longterok* (six stones), it is clear from the preceding narrative that they believe they are connected to the Chungli Aos. The Mongsen Aos made efforts to prevent the Chungli Aos from entering their territories for this reason. The discovery of headless bodies of Chungli Aos hunters by their hero, Shiluti, in the previous tale, serves as evidence of their opponents' head-hunting practices. Following the conquest of the Mongsen Aos by the Chungli Aos, the former were compelled to accept the terms and conditions set by the latter, resulting in the powerful Chungli Aos gaining authority over them.

Subsequently, a hierarchical organisation was established within Ao-Naga society through the institutions of marriage and kinship, with customary law and order governing village administration, politics, and economic activities, as well as streamlining moral and ethical aspects. The entire Ao community migrated westward from Chungliyimti, crossing the Dikhu River enroute to establishing settlements, as previously mentioned. The Aos eventually settled in Aonglenden (Mokokchung district), where they had ten boys. The settlement was initially named Soyim, but was later renamed Ungma after one of the *Unger* (Chiefs) was killed by a tiger there, combining the words *Ung* (chief) and *ma* (lost). Subsequently, the Aos left Soyim and journeyed to Koridang, a new location, before expanding to other areas within the present Ao nation. While Longkhum settlement was founded by one clan, the majority of the population settled in the Koridang Range. Sütsü and Kabza were established by one group, while Ungma was founded by another. These villages, situated within the Ongpangkong range, the largest of the six ranges inhabited by the Aos, served as the foundation for the creation of additional communities over time. The Aos are said to have driven out several early Konyak tribal inhabitants, including the Isangyonger, Nokranger, and Molunger clans, when they settled in the current regions (Mills 1926, 9). This is because these people are still remembered on numerous locations, and some of them have been assimilated into Ao society.

There is no historical record to trace the route of Ao migration and Ao traditional stories also do not go beyond *Longterok* (Ghosh 1979, 30). Nevertheless, for decades, historians and scholars maintained the belief that the Aos originated from six stones at Chungliyimti. Furthermore, it is crucial to also highlight that despite the traditional belief linking the Ao-Naga to *Longterok*, shifts in beliefs due to Christian influences and educational advancements have led to a divergence in interpretations regarding their mythical origins. The Mongsen group formed a study and research group in 1985 to learn more about the Mongsens and obtain a deeper grasp of the Ao origin (Mongsen Mongdang, Report, 1985).

During their journey, they visited all of Nagaland's bordering tribes. The Mongsen Aos are believed to have arrived in Nagaland via the lower Irrawaddy Valley around 300 B.C., while the Chungli Aos arrived by the upper Chindwin River around the same time, with their first settlement at Chungliyimti sometime between 100 and 125 A.D., as documented by Panger Imchen. According to W. C. Smith, Mongsen and Chungli had distinct identities until they coexisted in Chungliyimti. J. P. Mills suggests that the Mongsen arrived first, followed by the Chunglis. There are various perspectives and interpretations on this matter.

The Sumi and Lotha Nagas have names for the places that were once inhabited by the Aos. Legend has it that a group of Aos from Koridang ventured south to the current Sumi and Lotha area in search of better land. They resided in those areas for a period before returning north and reuniting with the Aos mainstream when suitable terrain became scarce. The Sumis dubbed the Aos *Julimi* when they attempted but failed to follow them. Some Aos are said to have traversed the Sumis' lands, and locations like Aochakilimi, Lumami, and Lotisami are believed to represent former Ao settlements. According to reports, the Mongsen group learned about the tribes' origins from elderly visitors. The Ao people were said to have once lived among the Yimkhiung tribe before migrating out, as per the Yimkhiung tribe's account. Upon arriving in Burma, they sought out hilly terrain. A group of individuals traveling from Khezhakeno to Eastern Sangtam coined the term Chungliyimti. They do not subscribe to the belief that Aos originated from a stone. Aos and Sangtams, according to the Sangtams, previously lived together in Chungliyimti. They say the Aos arrived from Burma, and that some passed through Japhü and settled in Jakhama village, while the other group remained in the Chakhesang area. Later, the Aos proceeded to leave the Sangtams. When the Aos decided to settle down in a village, the first thing they did was survey the area. They began by digging a hole in the ground and filling it with the same soil. The dugout earth was regarded infertile if it could not fill the hole, and fertile if it could fill the hole. The Aos were able to settle down and continue their cultivation in this manner (interview Otsufuba Longkumer, 73 years, Longkhum village, 18 December 2007).

Until today, oral traditions passed down through generations by word of mouth seem to be unique to the village of Chungliyimti in the Tuensang District. However, based on previous explanations, it is believed that all Aos originated from the eastern side. Many researchers suggest that the Aos migrated to the Mokokchung District (where Ao residents reside) from Myanmar (Burma). It is thought that they collected materials such as bones and precious stones while crossing rivers and streams, using them to create armlets, necklaces, conch shells, cowries, and other items. Tragically, many Aos perished when their villages and granaries were destroyed by fire. The canoes, commonly used by islanders during migration, are depicted on the long drums carved from massive wood. It was only upon reaching the village of Chungliyimti that the Ao society became fully organised, marking a period of social and political reformation for the Aos. Following the construction of essential infrastructure, six *morungs* (dormitories) representing the six units of village administration were established.

## ORIGIN OF THE CLANS: BIRDS, ANIMALS, AND THEIR REMAINS LIKE FEATHERS AND CELESTIAL BODIES LIKE SKY, CLOUDS, WIND WATERS

As discussed above, from the *Longterok* tradition it is evident that the Aos are of two (i) Chungli and (ii) Mongsen groups. The Pongen, the Longkumer, and the Jamir clans descended from the Chungli Aos and the Imchen, the Longchar and the Walling clans emerged from Mongsen Aos. From these two groups, they spread and founded many clans. Today there are several clans in the Ao areas. Some myths trace the evolution of different clans of the Aos from these major groups of Aos. The narrative 5 shows how clans were originated from celestial bodies like sun and moon which reflect the animistic perception of the tribes predominant in their origin stories.

The narrator recounted the tale of a child who was believed to have been blessed by the sun and moon, ensuring prosperity for generations to come. This story, rooted in actual events on the range, highlights the importance of ancestral lineage and the power of tradition among the Ao-Naga people. The narrator chose not to disclose the name of the clan descended from the sun and moon's child, as it is against customary law to divulge information that may cause harm or offense to other clans. This respect for privacy and sensitivity towards others' feelings is a fundamental aspect of Ao-Naga culture. The legacy of the blessed child and their descendants serves as a reminder of the enduring influence of tradition and the significance of ancestral connections within the community. It is a testament to belief in the divine and the power of heritage in shaping the destiny of individuals and clans alike.

The Ao worldview is rich with myths that explain the origins of their sub-clans. One such myth is Narrative 6, which tells the story of the Ozukumer Ao-clan, a sub-clan of Longkumer of *Longterok*. According to this myth, the Ozukumer clan traces its roots back to inanimate materials such as a feather and a stone. The name "Ozukumer" literally translates to "one who was transformed into a bird" in the Ao language, with "Ozu" meaning bird. This clan is believed to have descended from Pongtang, who was transformed from a bird's feather into a man and raised by Longkongla in Narrative 6. The Longkumer clan recognises the Ozukumer clan as one of its sub-clans. This tale is well-known among the Ao-Nagas, highlighting the intricate and fascinating origin stories that are passed down through generations. The Ozukumer clan's connection to both inanimate objects and birds adds a unique and mystical element to their lineage, showcasing the depth of Ao culture and tradition.

From the above discussion, it is evident (P. D. Stracey, 1968) that the greatest mystery is the origin of numerous Naga tribes, as each tribe has its own version of their history. All experts believe, however, that the Nagas are of Mongoloid ancestry. They have a large head, light skin, black hair, and yellowish eyes, and have a light complexion. Between the big rivers of the Brahmaputra in India and the Salween River in Myanmar, they have distinct tribes and sub-tribes with various customs and traditions. The upper reaches of China's Hwang-Ho River are thought to have been the Mongoloid people's first home. They then proceeded to South-East Asia before arriving in these mountains. The Nagas claim their origin from village Makhel (as mentioned in the myth of Tiger, spirit and man, Narrative No.1) a historical site in Senapati, Manipur District and also from Khezhakeno (as mentioned in the Myth of flat stone and Three brothers, Narrative No.2) in Chakhesang region. The Angami Nagas connected their descent directly from the man mentioned in the tiger, spirit, and man myth from where one of the sons diverted his way to Khezhakeno (origin of the flat slab). From this place, the remaining tribes like the Lotha, Sema, Rengma emerged. The parents who stayed back in Khezhakeno were the descendent Kezami village (Chakhesang Naga).

It must be emphasised that while historians and scholars spark debates over the accuracy of the *Longterok* mythic origin story, the Ao-Nagas have long upheld the legitimacy of the origin myth of *Longterok*. The stones (origin stones) are retained as a foundation in recollection of their settlement in Chungliyimti (now in Tuensang District) and as an identity marker, according to extensive research. Even though there are no ancient stories that reach beyond *Longterok*, there are oral recollections of their homeland and kin in the East. Aos believes they are related to tribes in Southeast Asian countries, and many researchers and writers maintain that the Aos arrived in the Ao region via Myanmar (Burma).

To sum up, the frequent inter-tribal conflicts and migrations among the Nagas in the past hindered the development of a sense of brotherhood and fraternity among the tribes. Instead, each migrant group required a distinct identification to maintain their lineage. Consequently, the various Naga tribes crafted their own creation myths to set themselves apart from one another. These myths linked their origins to both animate and inanimate elements of the terrestrial and celestial realms, reflecting their animistic beliefs. When the origins of social groups are shrouded in mystery, it is common for them to attribute their beginnings to mythical beings or deities. Thus, the Naga creation myths fall into the categories of parthenogenesis and autogenesis. In their narrative constructions, parthenogenesis (the origin of the clans as a result of the union of human beings and spirits) and autogenesis (self-transformation into several forms until achieving a final shape or form) are expressed. The following chapter examines the structural features of Ao-Naga folk narratives in order to see how narrative structures and identity constructions are linked.

# 4

# AO-NAGA NARRATIVE TYPOLOGY AND STRUCTURE: METAPHORS OF IDENTITY

The present chapter focuses on (i) how the oral narratives of the Ao-Nagas (personal narratives and folk narratives) endure their core strands of identity in their narrative motifs, the themes, and (ii) how the structure of the oral narratives mirror the social stratification and cultural values of the Ao-Nagas. The folk narratives in this chapter are analysed using the Proppian and Levi-Straussian structural models and are further examined through Derridean post-structural hermeneutical discourse and narrative inquiry. These concepts are presented sequentially to provide a comprehensive analysis of the folk narratives, engaging readers in the analytical process.

## TYPOLOGY OF FOLKTALES AND MOTIFS

Typology is a scientific classification and study of types or categories that are prevalent not only among people but also in any system, structure, function, culture, or society. The categorical study of any cultural product gives a greater understanding of the worldview and expressive behaviours of its producers. Folktales serve as cultural expressions of people and societies, showcasing their unique identities and traditions. Through the typological classification and analysis of folktales, we gain insight into how communities have preserved their distinctiveness and heritage across generations. This study also sheds light on the intricate balance between the esoteric and exoteric aspects of identity formation within human groups. In particular, the Ao-Naga folktales are categorised based on prevalent motifs that are deeply rooted in their society. By examining these tales, we can better understand the values, beliefs, and customs that have shaped the identity of the Ao-Naga people.

In Ao-Naga tradition, storytelling is not a skill possessed by all; only a handful are naturally gifted with the art of narration. Even among them, the male tellers outnumber the females. It is because in Ao-Naga society men have more opportunities for exposure in various aspects of social life (politico-economic and socio-religious and legal) than women. Conventionally, men who take part in village councils, *Putu Menden*, are supposed to know the cultural and traditional norms as well as the customary law and order of their society. Although asked to address issues related to their community's laws and customs, the women tellers would rather have the men speak for them. The women are cautious that if anything goes wrong in their renditions, they believe that it is tantamount to the violation of their norms. They believe that it is the domain of the men (interview Longrichila Longchar, 78 years, Longkhum village, on 20 December 2007). Hence the men act as the 'active bearers'[59] of the Naga tradition whereas the women remain as 'complementary' to them.

The Aarne–Thompson classification of folktales is being followed in the chapter. Antti Aarne published it in 1910; it was then translated and enlarged by Stith Thompson. His six-volume *Motif-Index of Folk-Literature* (1932–37) is a repertoire of knowledge and an international key to categorising the traditional material. It is known as *Aarne*

---

[59] The information was gathered in the field during group discussions with the people of Ao community.

*Thompson Tale Type Index.* Thompson used motifs, themes, and content rather than structures in the process of categorisation of tales.

Thompson defines a motif as, "the smallest element in a tale, having a power to persist in tradition" (Alan Dundes 1997: 195–202). Motif indexing is the process of breaking down a story into its smallest unit (motifs) and arranging these units into an organised structure. The resulting index enables scholars to compare folktales across cultures by similar motifs and serves as a story-finding aid and selective bibliography of folktales in single editions and collections. The motif index proper is often accompanied by several other indices that help access to it, such as a subject index or a tale title index. The book is a collection of indices that provide access to the primary components, the motifs, and is well known as the "motif index".

## MOTIFS IN AO-NAGA FOLKTALES

The motifs of folk narratives collected from the community are categorised in the light of the classification of Aarne–Thompson. In the following table 4.1 the narrative-motifs prevalent in Ao-Naga society are given.

| Narrative | Motif | Motif Index |
|---|---|---|
| 1. A boy who chooses his wife (Narrative no. 5 - A boy tests two girls to choose as his wife)<br>2. The embarrassing boy (Narrative no. 6 - A boy gets embarrassed because he fails all the tests given by the girl's family) | Character | H1569. Tests of character-miscellaneous |

| Narrative | Motif | Motif Index |
|---|---|---|
| 3. Improper marriage (Narrative no. 7 - Two lovers cannot not marry because the girl is married to the lover's elder brother) | Grief<br><br>Fate | F1041.21. Reactions to excessive grief. M302.2. Man's fate written on his skull |
| 4. Origin of tattooing (Narrative no. 1 - A tale of how the tattoo originated among the Ao-Nagas) | Tattooing | A1465.1. Origin of tattooing A1595. Origin of tattooing. |
| 5. Designs of tattoos (Narrative no. 2 - The Mongsen and Chungli girls are identified through their tattoos) | Tattoo | H55.3. Recognition by tattoo. |
| 6. Two girls and their hair (Narrative no. 3 - How the maintenance of hair neglects the work) | Equals | P310.8. Friendship possible only between equals |
| 7. A tree spirit who loves a girl (Narrative no. 4 - The lover of the girl transforms into a tree when morning comes) | Transformation | D215. Transformation: Man to tree |
| 8. The son who goes to death-land (Narrative no. 8 - The son realises that the land of death and land of mortals are very different) | Help Land | F403.2. Spirits help mortals<br><br>E481. Land of the dead |

| Narrative | Motif | Motif Index |
| --- | --- | --- |
| 9. Distribution of property (Narrative no. 3 - Father distributes the property of the mother to the daughters accordingly) | Property | A1585. Origin of Laws: division of property in a family |
| 10. *Menangsangla* and *Nokshiloba* (Narrative no. 4 - Both the man and woman are judged by the lord of judgment, *Meyutsungba*) | Punishments | E606.1. Reincarnation as punishment for sin. Q220. Impiety punished |
| 11. Revenge for a father's death (Narrative no. 5 - Two sons take revenge upon the death of the father) | Son | H1228.2. Son goes out to avenge his father's death. |
| 12. Devil and the old man (Narrative no. 6 - The old man kills a devil with his hand) | Devil<br><br>Killing | M219.4. Familiar devours whoever does not keep pact with the devil.<br>G303.20. Ways in which the devil kills people. |
| 13. The rich girl who becomes a spinster (Narrative no. 7 - The rich girl cannot marry because she is in love with a poor boy) | Poor<br><br>Pride | T91.5. Rich and poor in love<br>T91.5.1. Rich girl in love with a poor boy.<br>Pride brought low |

| Narrative | Motif | Motif Index |
|---|---|---|
| 14. Two lovers of the same clan (Narrative no. 8 - One boy and girl of the same clan are in love but due to strong customary law they give up their love.) | Exogamy | T131.5. Exogamy. Marriage only outside the group |
| 15. The Man who marries his cousin (Narrative no. 9 - A man who marries his paternal cousin realises that his marriage with his cousin sister is unnatural for him and divorces her) | Marrying | A1552.1. Why brothers and sisters do not marry |
| 16. A wife who plays competition with her husband (Narrative no. 11 - Wife is taught by the voice of spirit not to compete with her husband after divorce) | Heaven | F966. Voices from heaven (or from the air) |
| 17. Stepmother (Narrative no. 12 - Stepmother who treats differently when served food) | Food | Q65.1. Supplying food to ungrateful stepmother rewarded. |

| Narrative | Motif | Motif Index |
|---|---|---|
| 18. *Sungrochetla* who becomes a cuckoo bird (Narrative no. 13 - *Sungrochetla* is a supernatural being married to a mortal man) | Supernatural | T111. Marriage of mortals and supernatural beings |
| 19. A girl who turns into a bird (Narrative no. 15) | Transformation | D156. Transformation; Man to cuckoo |
| 20. Two brothers and a tiger (Narrative no. 16 - Two brothers kill a tiger) | Tiger | J1706.1. Tiger as a stupid beast. |
| 21. The cursed mango tree (Narrative 40 - The daughters of a rich man celebrate their father's plentiful harvest) | Work | J21.50. Idleness begets woe; work brings happiness |
| 22. *Tsüposang* and the animals (Narrative No. 2 – A man understands the language of the animals) | Men<br><br>Animal | A2433.2.4. Animals that live with men<br>B217. Animal language learned |
| 23. *Aluyimer* (farmer) Narrative no.4 - The farmer works hard in the fields to survive because he knows that fishing will not help them in times of famine) | Fisherman | J345.2. A man leaves farming for fishing when the water dries up, he goes hungry. |

| Narrative | Motif | Motif Index |
|---|---|---|
| 24. Lijaba, the creator of Ao terrains (Narrative no. 3 - Lijaba, the creator of the earth creates the Naga land) | Mythological motifs | A801. Earthborn of chaos. Greek: Grote I 4ff.<br>A605. Primeval chaos. |
| 25. *Lijaba's* spirit (Narrative no. 3 - Lijaba's spirit is sent to the earth so that people will worship him) | Visit | K1811. Gods (saints) in disguise visit mortals<br>F32. God visits earth |
| 26. The story of *Longkongla* (Narrative no. 5 - A woman takes revenge by killing all the children and villagers in the village) | Feathers<br><br>Feather | T536. Conception from feathers falling on a woman.<br>D437.3. Transformation: feather to person |

**Table 4.1:** Motifs in the Ao-Naga Folk Narratives (Source: Based on information collected during fieldwork).

Among the 40 tales (mentioned in Chapter two), only 26 tales fall under the Aarne-Thompson motif-index tale type. The reasons for this classification are elaborated upon below. In general, the Ao-Naga tales are very simple having a single motif. The major motifs as cited in the above table are transformation, exogamy, marrying, work, mythological, supernatural, devil, killed, character, fisherman, tiger, punishment, help, land, food, son, property, poor, pride, visit, equals, tattoo/tattooing, heaven, feathers, transformation, grief, fate, men, animal. Almost all these tale types or motifs of the tales are synonyms of the mundane and spiritual lives of the tellers as well as the community. The motif of 'transformation' is predominant in the motifs. Non-living entities (e.g., stones, rocks, etc.) are transformed into living entities (e.g., human beings, trees, flowers, etc) and vice versa (humans into stones, trees, animals). The Ao-Nagas community's deep connection with nature and the environment, along with their belief in a spiritual essence present in all living and non-living entities, is reflected in the motifs of their oral narratives. This animistic spiritual ideology shapes the cultural identity of the Ao-Nagas, emphasising their reverence for the natural world and the interconnectedness of all beings.

Some tales have more than one motif. For example, the Ao-Naga narrative No. 14: *The devil and the old man*, contains two motifs namely *devil* and *killed*. Thus, the Narratives, Nos. 8, 15, 33, 3, and 27 in the above table have two motifs. The occurrence of more than one motif in the folk narratives indicates the growing complexity in social phenomena and politico-economic formations and nature vs. culture relationships due to the interventions like inter-tribal warfare or exchange relationships among the other ethnic tribes of the region.

The redundancy of motifs of exogamy-endogamy, marriage and conjugal fidelity and tattooing depicted in Ao-Naga folk narratives reiterate the norms and values that are to be endured to retain the 'racial purity' of the respective clans of their society and thereby the community's identity. There are interesting motifs peculiar to Ao-Nagas that emphasise the presence of a metaphysical world that judges the good or bad deeds of the human beings on the earth after they die. Some motifs show how Ao-Nagas categorise the cosmos into two different realms: the worlds of the dead and of the living. The motifs on stepmother (Narrative no. 17) are prevalent in the tradition which indicates the re-marriage of men, a dominant feature of patriarchy in tribal societies. 'Revenge' motifs are significant in their oral narratives. The tribal societies survive and endure on internecine warfare among clans or groups. To keep up the fervour of militancy, a requisite to win battles, 'revenge' has to be developed as an instinct among men and women to save their 'community selves' from the threat of others' incursions. The 'revenge motifs' of Ao-Naga folktales reflect the tribal law and order, the 'an eye for an eye'. The folktale that features the motif of sibling rivalries primarily focuses on the relationships between sisters. The tribal economy is based on hunting and gathering or shifting cultivation, especially jhum cultivation among the Aos necessitated sometimes keeping the younger children at home with their elder children. In the absence of their parents, the elder sisters used to exploit the labour and services of their younger sisters. Interestingly, Ao-Naga narrative tradition is conspicuous by the absence of motifs on (i) in-laws' conflict, (ii) domestic violence, (iii) incest. The reasons are explained as follows:

i)    In Ao-Naga tradition the newly wedded couple from the day of their marriage should lead independent lives, managing their mundane activities on their own. The interference of in-laws from either side appears to be negligible. Hence there is not much scope for regular interaction that would lead to conflicts.

ii)   Though physical violence by men against their wives is not uncommon in the Ao- Naga society, the issues, in general, are considered as internal to their respective families. But when the problem exceeds the 'patience limit' of the partner, it gets settled by family elders and community councils. Fear of society and law keep the conflicts among the family members in low profile. Hence the motifs on domestic violence are scanty.

iii)  The motif on incest is not found in the Ao-Naga folk narratives since kinship relations like in any other society strongly condemn the practice as unethical and unscrupulous. Since the child-rearing practices of the Ao-Naga community give less scope for sibling conflicts, the problems related to incest are not visible. Though here and there such episodes exist in the society, the issue did not raise to the level of constructing lore upon it.

Thus, the tale types/motifs prevalent in the oral narratives of the Ao-Nagas stand as the icons of their identity. In the same way, the sequential patterning of the different events and the cause-and-effect relationship among different events reflect the structure of Ao-Naga society.

## STRUCTURE OF AO-NAGA ORAL NARRATIVES: IDENTITIES

The structure can be defined as a system consisting of units having definite relationships among themselves and at the same time to the whole; therefore, units and their functions are predictable. The function is the contribution which a partial activity makes to the total activities of which it is a part. The structure and functions are inseparably interwoven to give meaning not only to the teller but also to the target audience. Propp used the term 'function' to refer to the 'act' of the character which causes the progression of the tale. The functions of each of the characters are constant elements independent of how or by whom they are fulfilled, thus becoming the fundamental components of a tale. The functions of each tale are limited and always sequentially identical, even if some of the functions are absent. He formed rules for the plots of fairy tales, which can be summarised as follows: "there are a set number of events (or functions, of which there are 31) and character-roles (Dramatis Personae) that appear in tales, and, while not all appear in each tale, those that do appear must come in a certain order. These rules do not hold literally true in all tales (in many tales, functions occur out of order); however, they are a good structure through which to analyse most stories of any type".[60]

Lévi-Straussian structuralism claims that although the manifestations may be very different, the human mental processes are the same in all cultures. He holds that the mind unconsciously follows the social world. The use of the structuralist models of myth allows for the reduction of material studied to manageable levels. The dominant manner to accomplish this goal is based on the use of the following concepts: a) surface and deep structure, b) binary oppositions culture/nature, and c) mediation.

a) Surface and Deep Structure: The surface structure provides us with the narrative, the deep structure with an explication of the myth. This is accomplished by discovering the major binary opposition(s) in the deep structure.

b) Binary oppositions: Lévi-Strauss holds that the primitive mind always perceives their world in binaries — rich/poor, male/female, high/low, etc. These occur in nature and nature in the human mind. Nature and culture often function as a

---

[60] http://en.wikipedia.org/wiki/Vladimir_Propp. Accessed: 19 September 2011.

     binary opposition in tales. However, depending on the tale or myth, the binary opposition changes.

c) Mediation: A binary opposition can be mediated by finding a solution to the opposition created by the binary. The mediation to culture/nature binary opposition is that culture transcends nature. The structural analysis aims to mark how the content is organised and how the function is expressed, not to negate the existence of the function or the content.

Though structuralism achieves objectivity, its readings ignore the specificity of actual texts and treat them as if they were produced by some impersonal force or power and not as the result of human effort. Further, the individuality of the text disappears in favour of looking at patterns, systems, and structures. Structuralists like Russian formalists also propose that all narratives can be charted as variations on certain basic universal narrative patterns. The chief tenets of structuralism are:

a) The structure of language itself produces 'reality', i.e., one can think only through language, and therefore all perceptions of reality are framed and determined by the structure of language.

b) Language is a mode of expression, and the source of meaning is not an individual's experience of being, but learned from the system which governs what any individual can do within it.

c) Rather than seeing the individual as the centre of meaning, structuralism places 'structure' at the centre. It is the structure that originates or produces meaning, not the individual self. Language in particular is the centre of self and meaning.

Structuralism was critiqued by the deconstructionist Jacques Derrida because it overlooked the 'self' of the people who had produced the structures. Derrida holds two key points to the idea of deconstruction:[61] (i) all systems or structures have a 'centre', the point of origin, the thing that created the system in the first place and (ii) all systems or structures are created of binary pairs of oppositions, of two terms placed in some sort of relationship to each other. One part of that binary pair is always more important than the other, that one term is 'marked' as positive and the other as negative. Hence in the binary pair good/evil, good is valued. Evil is subordinated to good. Derrida argues that in all binary-pair works, the first term is always valued over the second. Moreover, Derrida associates an opposition of speech and writing with the binary pair of the opposition of metaphysical presence and absence. He holds that *speech* prevails over the *writing* as it gets associated with *presence*, and both are favoured over *writing* and *absence*. Derrida called such privilege of speech and presence as logocentrism. He advocated that the pair of binaries cannot exist without reference to the other. For example, light (as *presence*) is defined as the *absence* of darkness, goodness in the *absence* of evil. Deconstruction never sought the reversal of hierarchies implied in binary pairs — to make evil favoured over good, unconscious over consciousness, and feminine over masculine. But it wants to erase the boundaries (the slash) between oppositions, hence, to show that the values and order implied by the opposition are also not rigid. His method of deconstruction is as follows: "Find a binary opposition. Show how each term, rather than being the polar opposite of its paired term, is actually part of it. Then the structure or opposition which kept them apart collapses, as in the binaries of nature and culture.

Deconstruction is a combination of construction and destruction — the idea is that one need not simply construct a new system of binaries, with the previously subordinated term on top, nor destroy the old system — rather, one may deconstruct the old system by showing

[61] Derrida and Deconstruction: http://courses.nus.edu.sg/course/elljwp/ deconstruction.htm. For further readings: Peggy Kamuf, (ed.), *Derrida: A Reader*, Hemel Hempstead: Harvester, 1991. A collection of essays (including one by Derrida himself) about Derrida may be found in Wood, David, (ed.), *Derrida: A Critical Reader*, London: Blackwell, 1992.

how its basic units of structuration (binary pairs and the rules for their combination) contradict their logic.

In the light of the above discussion, when Ao-Naga oral narratives are subjected only to Proppian and Levi-Straussian structural analyses, the narrative structure reveals a syntagmatic and paradigmatic dimension of the identity formations. The dimension of deconstruction has to be added to give a holistic picture of how narrative structures echo the identity of the narrators and their communities. The perspective of the narrator's self (personal and community) in analysis and interpretation of the oral narratives negotiate the pairs in the binaries from the respective cultural perspective and erase the boundaries between the narrator and narrative to establish a narrative identity.

Keeping in view the postmodern and poststructuralist discourse that contributed to the emergence of perspectival studies, D. Clandinin and F. Connelly (2000, 3) developed a narrative method of inquiry in which narrative is used as a method as well as an object study in the interpretation of cultures. Narrative as a method describes across time and space the various ways in which actors rely on narrative form in interpreting and making sense of their worlds. The narrative is also studied as an object to study social life. Here the narrative is used as a fundamental social concept to denote the process by which people communicate their understanding of the world. Further narrative inquiry emphasises syntagmatic, paradigmatic, and cross-sectional dimensions of narrative and deconstructs and reconstructs meanings of the metaphors from the viewpoint of the narrators and their community. In the present context, narrative inquiry is employed to analyse oral narratives to give a holistic picture of how structures reveal the identities.

Narrative inquiry refers to any study that uses or analyses narrative materials (Durga, 2007). It is a dynamic and dialogical process approach that construes life experiences, both personal and social, in relevant and meaningful ways. The act of creating and telling a story is a heuristic as well as hermeneutic inquiry. It is heuristic because in the creation of a story, the qualities, meanings, and essences of universally unique experiences are portrayed (C. Moustakas, 1990, 13). It is hermeneutic because it is a meaning-making and interpretative process operating at two levels: (1) creation of general understanding through the use of symbolic systems, wherein every act of comprehension is by nature hermeneutic (2) involves the systematic use of hermeneutic interpretation as a strategy to approach participants' meaning in a given social interaction. In light of the above theoretical discussion, Ao-Naga folk narratives are analysed to show how their structures reveal the dynamics of the social construction of the narrators' identities.

Considering the discussion above, the narratives can be analysed from three dimensions (Durga, 2007, 102): (1) The action as it happened in its actual chronological sequence (the story); (2) the story's causal structure (plot); and (3) the sequence of events as ordered in the narrative by the narrator (discourse). In this section, a structural analysis of the oral narrative (i) Revengeful sons (*Mangyangba jabaso*) is done as an example to show how identities get reflected in the narrative structures. The tale was told by a village councillor, Tsükdinungba Longkumer (75), hailing from Mokokchung District, the abode of the Ao-Nagas.

## ANALYSIS OF THE NARRATIVE: THE STORY OF THE REVENGEFUL SONS (*MANGYANGBA JABASO*)

The folktale "Revengeful Sons" (*Mangyangba jabaso*) was collected from Tsükdinungba Longkumer, a 75-year-old resident of Changtongya village in Mokokchung District. Longkumer is a highly respected elder, *Oala* in the community, having served as the Chairman (*Menden*) of the Village Council (*Putu Menden*) for 30 years. Throughout his life, Longkumer has built up an impressive repertoire of experiences, serving both his clan and the Village Council in various capacities. He has witnessed the changing dimensions of Ao-Naga folklife over three generations and is well-versed in the customary laws that govern social and cultural practices in the village. His knowledge goes beyond the Aos as he navigates through different Naga tribes, resolving conflicts in various villages. A skilled narrator and preserver of tradition, Longkumer shares stories that often highlight the importance of gender roles and the consequences of punishments for crimes.

Longkumer's personal journey reflects the cultural shifts within the community, from his early adherence to animistic beliefs that delayed his marriage until he embraced Christianity at the age of 23. He recounts experiences dealing with witch doctors/sorcerers (*arasentsür*) during times of illness, demonstrating the complex spiritual practices that have shaped his life.

Overall, Longkumer's narratives offer valuable insights into the Ao-Naga culture and traditions, making him a cherished source of local wisdom and history. Here is one of the many tales recounted by him while the author was conducting fieldwork. The first step in the narrative analysis is the action as it happened in its actual chronological sequence (the story):

## NARRATIVE 7: THE STORY OF THE REVENGEFUL SONS (*MANGYANGBA JABASO*)

In the village of Koridang, there resided a family consisting of a mother and her two sons. Tragically, when the sons were young, their father was killed by members of the Sangtam tribe who also took the boys away. As the sons grew older, they yearned for answers about their father's fate, prompting them to repeatedly question their mother. Her response was always the same - to wait until they were mature enough to handle the truth. Upon reaching the ages of twelve and thirteen, the mother decided it was time to reveal the identity of their father's killer. She instructed her sons to sharpen their daos, a type of large machete used as a weapon, and presented them with a challenge. If they could cut a dried cane rope in one swift motion, she would disclose the name of the perpetrator. The sons successfully completed the task, leading their mother to disclose the entire story of their father's demise. Following their mother's guidance, the sons infiltrated the killer's household under the guise of offering their services. They gained his trust over the years, patiently waiting for the opportune moment to exact their revenge. When the time came, they lured the old man to a fishing trip and ultimately ended his life in the forest. Through their mother's wisdom and their own patience and determination, the sons were able to avenge their father's death and eliminate their lifelong enemy. The tale of their journey from grief to justice serves as a testament to the power of perseverance and strategic thinking.


## PLOT STRUCTURE


The plot is a literary term defined as the events that make up a story, particularly as they relate to one another in a pattern, in a sequence, through cause and effect, or by coincidence. The narrator is skilfully present in such a way that the patterning of events in the plot of their renditions would accomplish some artistic and emotional effect and thereby reflect their personal and community selves. Aristotle, in his book, *The Poetics*, states that plot structure has "a beginning, middle and an end". But it is much more than simply the telling of events one after another. A plot needs a motivating purpose to drive the story to its resolution, and a connection between these events.

The story (narrative 7) begins with a 'complete family' comprising husband, wife, and children. A villain from the Sangtam tribe creates havoc in the family by killing the father who belongs to the Ao tribe. The responsibility falls upon the mother to take the role of father.

The middle part of the story revolves around the mother. She brings up the children with care. She puts her sons to a test that they should cut the log in one shot by a word. When they succeed in that test, the mother reveals the secret of the death of the father and schemes a plan to kill the enemy. When the sons leave home for the place of villain, the middle portion ends.

The end of the story begins with the strategic behaviour of the son with the enemy and finally concludes with the killing of the villain on the way from the forest to the fishing pond. Thus, the Aristotelian's plot structural analysis gives a picture of how an action/event leads to several events in the storyline but does not unfold interpretation of deeper meanings attached to the characters in the narrative.

## ANALYSIS OF THE FOLKTALE THROUGH THE SYNTAGMATIC APPROACH

In this approach, the 'Proppian Functions' depicted in the previous folktale are first analysed and subsequently, the causal relationship between events in the tale is studied by sequentially arranging different events that lead the story in 'Moves'[62].

The story or folktale is interwoven among four characters, the **victim**, the father who was killed, the **villain**, the old man who murdered the father, and the mother who enacts as the **dispatcher** and the **donor**. She empowers her children with revenge and the ability to take revenge upon her husband's death. The fourth is the **hero**, the sons' character who realises their mother's wish of cutting the head of their father's killer.

The story begins with the **initial situation** of the family, in which husband and wife live happily with two sons. The next function is the **violation**. It is marked by the entry of the **villain** who kills the father and took the dead of the father. A **lack** in the family is created with the death of the father, realising the function of **abstention**. The mother passes (**meditation**) the information to her sons about the person who killed their father. The story follows the function of a **donor sequence**, in which the sons are tested to prove their valour that makes them triumphant over the villain. The **first function of the donor** is thus served. The sons (**heroes**) react to the **donor** (mother) and leave the home (**departure**) to stay with the old man, the **villain**. The boys **struggle** to stay and work with the old man for many years and killed in direct combat and there is their **victory** of defeating the villain (**liquidation**). Thus, the sons brought satisfaction to the mother because the task was resolved (**solution**).

The causal relationship between the events in the plot that develop the storyline are analysed and represented in two 'moves'.

---

[62] According to Propp's theory of narrative, moves are narrative functions or actions that unfold within a story. Propp identified 31 moves, which represent recurring patterns or elements found in traditional Russian fairy tales.

The plot or sequence of events of the story is shown in the following table.

| S. No. | Move I | S. No. | Move II |
|---|---|---|---|
| 1. | There was a family. | 1. | The sons stay with the old man. |
| 2. | The father was killed by members of the Sangtam tribe who also took his dead body | 2. | They work for the old man. |
| 3. | The mother takes care of her sons. | 3. | They take the old man for fishing. |
| 4. | The sons inquire about their father. | 4. | They take revenge and kill the old man. |
| 5. | The mother examines her sons' strengths. | 5. | They realise the mother's wish (taking revenge upon their father's death). |
| 6. | The mother tells the sons who killed their father. | | |
| 7. | The mother sends her sons to stay with the old man. | | |

**Table 4.2:** Analysis of the plot

The analysis shows that the plot structure has two moves, having a character of father, mother, old man/enemy and sons/children. Move I begins with the lack created in the family with the death of the father by an enemy and ends with the 'departure' of the sons to the enemy place to take revenge for their father's death.

The second move begins with the stratagem of the sons to take revenge and ends triumphantly with the killing of the enemy. The lack created in the family, exclusively to the mother had been **liquidated** by replacing the same 'father figure' (the villain) in the other family. **Revenge is the medium of liquidation of lack.**

When coming to the characters, two forming a 'dyad' interact per scene. Dyads are any two characters interacting with each other at a given time in any particular scene (Durga 2007, 106). The following table shows the interaction of the 'dyads' in the tale:

| S. No | Move I | S. No | Move II |
|---|---|---|---|
| 1. | Father/ mother / children | 1. | Sons/old man (enemy) |
| 2. | Father/villain | | |
| 3 | Mother/sons | | |

**Table 4.3:** Dyad interaction (of characters)

In Move I, all four characters appear interacting to construct the storyline. The story begins with a 'triad', the interaction among the characters of the father, mother, and children in the happy family. It is followed by father and villain dyad, in which the latter vanquishes and kills the former. This action ignites a desire for revenge in the mother's mind, propelling the story forward to the next pivotal event: the mother imparting her training to her sons. It develops as a dialogue with the dyad mother/sons. In Move II, only one dyad, that is, the sons and the enemy interact with one another. In the combat between two characters, the latter dies at the hands of the former. In Move I, there is only one female character and the other three characters are male. In Move II, a single dyad containing two male characters leads the story. Thus, on the whole, the story contains male and female characters in a 3:1 ratio and appears to be male-centered.

## PARADIGMATIC STRUCTURAL ANALYSIS OF AN AO-NAGA MYTH

Claude Levi-Strauss views myths as stemming from a human need to make sense of the world and to resolve cultural dilemmas. These dilemmas are embodied in the structure of myths, which is made up of binaries or opposites, such as good-bad, night-day. For Levi-Strauss, myths are a kind of universal language. While the events of myths vary, the basic structures, like grammar, are similar in myths worldwide — because people are similar.


## NARRATIVE 6: THE STORY OF LONGKONGLA


Longkongla was a righteous woman who lived in Chungliyimti village. She was a member of the Longkumer family. She was a just and upright woman who was hospitable and loved children and everyone on the earth. A male hornbill (*tenem ozü*) passed her by one day as she was weaving her cloth in her courtyard. "*I wish the hornbill dropped one of its feathers so that I can wear it to the Moatsü festival*", she wished at the time. The hornbill then let go of one of its feathers. She was pleased when she saw the feather. The feather remained in her *kettsu* (cane mat box). She discovered the next day that the feather had transformed into a sharpening stone. She kept the stone in the fore room at the entrance to her house. That stone was soon converted into a shattered bamboo basin. She tossed it out the window. She realised the broken bamboo basin had transformed into a baby boy later that night. He was in tears. She raised him as a foster child and gave him the name *Pongtang*, which means "the one whom everyone attempts to carry".

He matured into a strong and handsome young man who was admired by all women, young and old. Some of the villagers were jealous of the boy. He was taken fishing one day and was killed. After learning of the tragedy, Longkongla resolved to exact vengeance by killing all the residents. She intended to kill the children first, then the villagers who would come to her house seeking vengeance. She killed a huge pig and cooked it one day when all the people were out in the field. She invited all of the children to the feast. She closed the doors and set fire to it while they were eating. Except for one boy who fled and informed the village, all the children were burned to death. When word of the tragedy reached the village's chief (*ungr*), the council ordered all his villagers to stay at home and execute Longkongla. After learning of their plan, she surrounded herself with grains — rice, millet, soybeans, and maize — and waited for the villagers to arrive while weaving her cloth. All the men later met with their *dao* (machete). They slipped on the rice grains and beans as they approached her with the dao and fell. As a result, Longkongla killed everyone with her sword, a weaver's baton (*alem*). She was alone by the time nightfall arrived. She couldn't live on her own. She asked the god of heaven (*anintsüngba*) to lift her to heaven as she no longer wished to remain on earth. The god told her that he would lift her to heaven only if she forgot all her attachments, possessions, and belongings on the earth. Moreover, she could not look down even if her kith and kin called for her. God further told her that if she did not follow these conditions she would be dropped from heaven. She promised him that she would not look down. The god stretched the rope from heaven to lift her. But halfway to heaven, she heard all the cries of her cows, dogs, pigs, chickens, and goats. As their voices grew louder, she looked down because she missed them. The moment she looked down she was dropped to the earth and turned into a rock. Her son who was born from a hornbill feather became the originator of the *Ozukumer* clan of the Aos.

The above myth can be divided into mythemes[63] and organised both in terms of syntagmatic and paradigmatic style as shown in the below table. When reading a story in a syntagmatic manner, one can gain a meaningful understanding of its content. Conversely, approaching the text paradigmatically allows for the identification of binaries based on similarities and differences.

---

[63] Mythemes refers to the smallest meaningful units of mythological narratives and are usually identified by breaking down myths into their constituent parts. By deconstructing myths into mythemes, Levi-Strauss aimed to uncover these underlying patterns and understand the deep meaning and functions of myths in society.

| 1 | 2 | 3 | 4 | 5 |
|---|---|---|---|---|
| Hornbill feather turns to stone. Stone turns to a broken bamboo basin. Bamboo turns to a baby boy. | | | | |
| | The boy is reared and loved by the woman (mother) | The boy is killed by the villagers | | |
| | | Woman kills the children of the village | | |
| | | Woman kills the villagers | | |
| | The woman loved her reared animals like cows, pigs, chicken etc. | | The woman turns to stone | |
| | | | | The emergence of clan claimed from the boy. |

Table 4.4: Levi-Straussian way of organising mythemes

1= Autogenesis origin of the community through boy (representing life)

2= Woman's immense love for boy and animals (overrating of blood relations)

3= Boy killed by children/villagers and woman, in turn, killing them (underrating of blood relations)

4= Autogenesis origin of stone (representing lifelessness)

5= emergence and continuity of clan (denial of Autogenesis origin of the community)

Binaries in the above myth can be seen as 1:4 ∷ 2:3

Autogenesis life x Autogenesis lifelessness

∷

Overrating of blood relations x Underrating of blood relations

In the above binaries column 1 represents life as the boy is born and column 4 represents death as the woman turns to a stone which is a state of lifelessness. Therefore 1 and 4 are binaries as a representation of life and lifelessness.

Column 2 represents the immense love a woman has for a boy and animals, leading to what can be described as an 'overrating of blood relations'. The woman's love for the boy is so intense that she seeks revenge on those who caused his death. Additionally, her deep affection for animals and possessions prevents her from entering heaven, despite her desire to do so. As a result, she is cast back to earth as a stone. Column 3 shows killing as a distinct feature wherein the boy is killed by the other children of the village and hence the woman takes revenge by killing the children first by setting fire to the hut and later killing all the villagers by the sword and therefore it represents 'underrating of blood relations'.

Column number 5 is a denial of Autogenesis origin of the community because the myth is silent about the marriage of the boy or the progeny of the boy. Therefore, it is a basic denial of the autogenesis origin of the community and also establishing the patriarchy form of the social system by showing the death of a woman who brought up the boy and by simply attributing the lineage to the boy. Therefore, the myth addressed the issue of life and death and resolved that the existing phenomenon of the community's non- autogenesis origin and patriarchy is to be socially validated.


## DISCOURSE


When examining structural analyses through the lens of narrative inquiry and Derridean epistemology, a comprehensive understanding of narrative discourse is revealed. The narrative discourse throws a flood of light on who narrated the story, from whose perspective it is narrated, the socio-cultural context of its narration, and on how the narrative represents the identities of the people and communities who produced the narrative tradition.

The narrator, Tsükdinungba Longkumer, hails from Changtongya village in Mokokchung District, where a large population of Ao-Naga resides. With over three decades of experience as the head of a village council, he has encountered numerous challenges and triumphs in both his personal and professional life. Longkumer has navigated through various conflicts, both within and between tribes and villages, using his wisdom and leadership skills to resolve issues affecting the lives of individuals and families. His vast experiences have shaped him into a respected and knowledgeable figure within his community. For him, his personal life is not much separated from his official affairs. As head of the village council, his prime duty is to regulate the social roles of the people and reiterate the norms and values of the community. In ancient tribal societies, life was often precarious, with families' frequently experiencing loss due to the absence of male members (sons or fathers) in constant warfare. In these challenging circumstances, village councils played a crucial role in guiding and supporting women, particularly widows, as they navigated their changing gender roles. Overall, Ao-Naga women are known for their bravery and strong work ethic. They possess a deep understanding of the traditions and principles of their community. Even in challenging circumstances, they remain steadfast in their duties and work tirelessly to preserve their clan or tribal heritage. In times of conflict or loss, when male members are unable to fulfil their roles, the women step up to raise and educate the children, instilling in them a sense of justice and determination to seek retribution against those who have wronged them. This emphasis on revenge plays a central role in shaping the gender dynamics within tribal society. It gets reflected in the practice of headhunting among Ao-Nagas. Headhunting was a ritualistic practice in which warriors would cut off the heads of their enemies and bring them back to their village as a symbol of revenge.

This act was seen as heroic and avenging, bringing honour to the individual who carried it out and elevating their status within their community. Women in these societies played a crucial role in instilling a sense of community pride and unity among the younger generation by recounting tales of bravery and heroism. The narrator's identity with the narrative gets reflected in many ways. As a person taking the role of a councillor, he passes the message to the people about the duty of a woman in a conflict situation at family as well as at community levels. For the tribal groups the personal and community identities merge in their social lives; killing the enemy of a family tantamount to the elimination of their opponent clan/group. The narrator converges his professional and personal experiences in the narrative and thus established the narrative identity.

Regarding the nature of the narrative 7, it may initially seem to be male-cantered. However, upon closer examination, it becomes evident that all male characters are actually centred around the female protagonist, who serves as the focal point of the story. This gender construction highlights the importance of the woman as the cornerstone of the home. The tale illustrates the societal expectations placed upon a Naga woman in terms of upholding family and community norms.

The discussions with the narrator enabled the researcher to interpret the story from the perspective of the Ao-Naga among whom such tales are widespread.

The narrative 7 serves as a symbolic representation of the evolving economic practices throughout various seasons, including hunting/gathering, agriculture, and fishing. Within the story, the sons' labour alongside the antagonist in the agricultural fields, then accompany him on fishing expeditions once the harvest season has concluded.

This illustrates the strategic utilisation of available resources during different times of the year. Moreover, the sons are eventually sent to work as slaves on the villain's farm, highlighting the emergence of slavery coinciding with the establishment of settled agricultural practices such as terrace cultivation (*panikhets*). The mother devises a cunning plan to eliminate the enemy, opting for a more indirect approach rather than instructing her sons to directly confront and kill the villain. She imbues her children with a thirst for vengeance and the physical prowess needed to carry out the deed. The mother only reveals the truth about the father's fate once she is confident that her sons are capable of exacting revenge. The test she sets for them, requiring them to sever a cane rope with a single knife stroke, serves as a symbolic assessment of their strength and readiness. This act mirrors the precision and skill required in traditional headhunting practices, where an enemy's head must be cleanly severed in one swift motion. Ultimately, the method of dispatching the enemy in the story differs from traditional headhunting, resembling instead the strategic trapping of animals in the forest. This nuanced approach adds depth and complexity to the narrative, underscoring the intricate interplay between vengeance, strength, and cunning in the face of adversity.

The following observations are made in the chapter. The study of tale types/motifs of the Ao-Naga oral narratives reveals their identity through their belief system, norms and values, and cultural practices in the society. In general, the tales are very simple having a single motif, but some tales contains more than one motif. The transformation motif is found dominant. The non-living gets transformed into living and *vice versa*. This shows their animistic features that were prevalent among the Aos. The tale types/motifs prevalent in the Ao-Naga oral narratives such as exogamy-endogamy, marriage, patriarchy, headhunting, life after death and agricultural practices like *jhum* cultivation stand as the icons of their identity. Through the study of the tale types/motifs, it is also observed that there are certain areas that are not prevalent: in-laws' conflict, domestic violence, and incest which shows that all cultures are not the same.

The structural analyses conducted by Proppian and Lévi-Straussian reveal a complex interplay between syntagmatic and paradigmatic dimensions within narrative identity formations. While their analyses provide insight into the sequential patterning of events and cause-and-effect relationships, they fall short in conveying the deeper meanings inherent in narratives. When viewed through the lens of Derridean deconstruction, structural analyses offer a more comprehensive understanding of narratives when approached from a narrative inquiry perspective. What may initially appear as a simple story or folktale gains depth and complexity when its structure is interpreted through narrative inquiry. By combining the structural analyses of Proppian and Lévi-Straussian with Derridean deconstruction, a holistic interpretation emerges that sheds light on the construction of identity within the narrative. This collaborative approach enriches the narrative experience by uncovering layers of meaning that may have otherwise remained hidden.

# 5

# CONCLUSION

The lore of the Nagas encompasses a wealth of knowledge, beliefs, and customs that have helped the community maintain a sense of self amidst changing times. It is truly a treasure trove of their history, offering a diverse range of genres such as folk narratives, songs, proverbs, riddles, performing arts (music, dances, drama, painting, arts), and extensive material culture. These cultural expressions not only reflect the unique identity of the Naga tribal communities but also provide valuable insights into their collective past. Thus, through a profound reading and analysis of the lore, we gain a deeper understanding of the complexities of the Naga identity, society, and spiritual traditions that continue to resonate within the community. As such, the task of preserving the cultural heritage of the Nagas relies heavily on documenting their lore, which offer historical context and valuable insights into their myths, beliefs, and social structures. Such an effort serves as a portal unveiling the complex and multifaceted tribal culture that never fails to intrigue both researchers and readers.

With a particular emphasis on the Ao-Naga community, the current book *Oral Narratives and the Ao Nagas: A Journey of Identity Construction* explores the personal and folk accounts relayed by members of both genders within a variety of cultural environments, illuminating the societal challenges that have influenced their sense of self throughout history. The Ao-Nagas, much like other oral societies, rely on their rich lore and expressive traditions to navigate the complexities of their world. These traditions have been passed down verbally through generations, serving as a cornerstone of their cultural heritage. By compiling the narratives of the Ao-Nagas into one cohesive collection, this book plays a crucial role in preserving their rich heritage of oral storytelling. It ensures that these cultural treasures are not only documented but also passed down to future generations. Taking a comprehensive look at Ao-Naga folk narratives and their structural features, the book studies the intricate relationship between storytelling, identity construction, and cultural memory within their community. Besides, through an in-depth analysis of the narratives and oral traditions of the Ao-Nagas, researchers and readers alike would be able to gain profound insights into the beliefs, values, and customs of this indigenous community. By referencing historical encounters between the Naga people and the British administrators-ethnologists, the book also gives a glimpse into the early initiatives taken to explore and record information about this unique tribal community. This historical context is crucial for tracing the development of Naga studies and the pioneering work undertaken to understand and record this tribal community. Overall, this book, sharing the multitude of narrative accounts with a wider audience, aims to promote intercultural dialogue and fosters appreciation for the diversity of human experiences and storytelling traditions.

The myths and legends discussed in the book provide insights into the Ao-Naga's spiritual beliefs and cosmology, enriching our understanding of Ao-Naga mythology and their perception of the world. Through the stories shared, we also gain insights into the social structure, kinship systems, and customary laws of the Naga tribes. Understanding these aspects is essential for comprehending the intricate societal dynamics within Ao-Naga communities. In addition to valuable insights into the folklore narratives, myths and communal philosophies of the Ao-Nagas, the book provides readers with valuable knowledge on their origins and migration. In other words, giving importance to the diverse array of origins among the Naga tribes, especially the Ao-Nagas, the book highlights the individual narratives that distinguish and define each group within the larger Naga community. The examination of origin and migration narratives gives insight into the Naga people's understanding of their own origins, providing a foundation for Naga identity and a sense of belonging within their communities. The myths of parthenogenesis and autogenesis illuminate the intricate origins and identities of the Ao-Naga clans. The book also examines how inter-tribal conflicts and migrations have impacted the evolution of Naga society, obstructing the creation of a cohesive sense of brotherhood and fraternity. All these historical factors have played a pivotal role in shaping the unique cultural identities and narratives of the various Naga tribes.

By examining the myths and beliefs of the Ao-Naga people, the book sheds light on the animistic worldview and spiritual connections that form the foundation of Ao-Naga society. The narratives that connect human origins to celestial and terrestrial realms reflect the deeply ingrained cultural beliefs and practices of the Ao-Nagas. The book further examines the complex structure of the folk narratives of the Ao-Nagas through the utilisation of various models and concepts. It initiates by categorising the folk narratives based on prevalent motifs deeply ingrained in Ao-Naga society. The analysis continues to study the typology of folktales and motifs, with the aim of offering a comprehensive understanding of the worldview and expressive behaviour of the Ao-Naga people. The Proppian and Levi-Straussian structural models are employed to dissect the folk narratives, with a focus on the action unfolding in its chronological sequence, the causal structure of the story (plot), and the sequence of events as narrated by the storyteller (discourse). In addition, the narratives are scrutinised through Derridean post-structural hermeneutical discourse and narrative inquiry, enabling a deeper exploration of the social stratification and cultural values of the Ao-Nagas. The analysis shows how the structures of the narratives mirror the dynamics of the social construction of the narrators' identities, offering insights into the values, beliefs, and customs that have moulded the identity of the Ao-Naga people. The core strands of identity among the Ao-Nagas, as explored in the book, are intricately woven into their oral traditions. These narratives are rich with motifs that symbolise various aspects of their culture, such as transformation, exogamy, marriage, work, mythology, the supernatural, devilry, character traits, and interactions with nature and animals. These motifs serve as allegorical representations of both the everyday and the spiritual dimensions of life within the Ao-Naga community, pointing out their profound connection to the natural world and their belief in the interconnectedness of all living beings. It offers insights into the societal norms and values that shape the Ao-Naga community, including practices like exogamy and endogamy, marriage customs, patriarchal structures, historical traditions like headhunting, and agricultural techniques like jhum cultivation, all of which serve as pillars of their cultural identity. Within the narrative there also lies an examination of the value placed on preserving racial purity and clan lineage, touching upon themes of conflict with in-laws, domestic disagreements, and various trials that challenge the unity of Ao-Naga society.

Understanding the Ao-Nagas perspective on the metaphysical realm requires examining their narratives, which vividly depict concepts of judgment in the afterlife and the division of the cosmos between the realms of the living and the deceased. In addition, gender dynamics in the Ao-Naga society are heavily influenced by the art of storytelling. Men predominantly hold the role of storytellers, as they are more exposed to various aspects of social life, including politico-economic, socio-religious, and legal matters. This is primarily due to their active participation in village councils, where they are expected to possess knowledge about cultural norms, traditional practices, and customary laws. To put it concisely, the preference for male storytellers in Ao-Naga society reflects the prevailing societal norms and gender roles, where men are expected to be the primary conveyors of cultural knowledge and traditions.

In contrast, women may be proficient storytellers, but they are overlooked for this specific role. Similarly, they tend to give precedence to men explaining community laws and traditions, believing that men are better suited for such tasks. Despite this, numerous narratives celebrate the bravery and sincerity of Ao-Naga women, depicting their essential contributions in safeguarding their clan's legacy and perpetuating the traditions and beliefs of their families and communities. Through the lens of these narrative accounts, the perseverance and devotion of Ao-Naga women stand out, exemplifying sources of power and virtue in their society.

Integrating all the analyses and results into a cohesive whole, the Ao-Nagas, as a unique folklore community, draw strength from purposefully utilising verbal and non-verbal folklore genres in their daily lives to solidify their identity amidst the challenges of modernity and globalisation. This intentional preservation of traditional folklore practices serves as a powerful tool for the Ao-Nagas to assert their cultural heritage and resist the homogenising forces of contemporary society. In its entirety, this book serves as a humble endeavour to present a unique outlook on Ao-Naga culture, offering researchers, folklorists and anthropologists a deeper understanding of the community's way of life, societal norms and historical accounts. By restating, the narrative accounts compiled in this book are designed to function as a vital asset for cultural preservation, advancing academic study, and promoting cross-cultural understanding and appreciation.

# SELECTED BIBLIOGRAPHY


Aier, Anungla, Studies on Naga Oral Tradition (Volume.1) Memories and Telling of Origin Myth and Migration, Dimapur: Heritage Publishing House, 2018.

Aier, I. Bendangangshi & I.T. Apok Aier, *The Religion of the Ao Nagas*, Guwahati, 1990.

Ao, Temsula, "Identity and Globalization: A Naga Perspective", in *Globalization and Tribes of Northeast India*, A quarterly newsletter Folklife from National Folklore Support Centre, Serial No.22, July, 2006, pp. 6-7.

Bareh, H., *Nagaland District Gazetteers Kohima*, Sree Saraswaty Press Limited, 1970.

Clandinin, D. Jean & F. Michael Connelly, "Narrative Inquiry: Experience and Story "in *Qualitative Research*, San Francisco: Jossey-Bass Publishers, 2000.

Clark, M.M, *A Corner in India*, Guwahati: Christian Literature Centre, (Reprinted and Published), 1978.

Dundes, Alan, "The Motif-Index and the Tale Type Index: A Critique", *Journal of Folklore Research*, Vol. 34, No. 3 (Sep. - Dec., 1997), pp. 195-202.

Dundes, Alan, *Folklore matters*, Knoxville: The University of Tennessee Press, 1989.

Durga, P. S. Kanaka, "Women and Social Identity in Folktales: Narrative Inquiry", *Kakatiya Journal of women's Studies* (BI ANNUAL), Vol. I. September, No.2, 2007

Durga, P.S. Kanaka, "Women and Social Identity in Folktales: Narrative Inquiry", *Kakatiya Journal of women's Studies* (BI ANNUAL), Vol. I. 2007.

Eliade, Mircea, *Myth and Realty*, London: George Allen and Unwin ltd., 1963.

Ghosh, B.B., *Nagaland District Gazetteers; Mokokchung* District; Kohima, Published by Government of Nagaland,

Horam, M., *Naga Polity*, New Delhi: B.R. Publishing Co. 1975.

Imchen, Mepolila. Oral narration. Longkhum village, December 20, 2007. Narrative 29.

Imchen, Panger, *Ancient Ao Naga Religion and Culture*, New Delhi: Har Anand Publication, 1993.

Jamir, Imolemba. Oral narration. Ungma village, December 19, 2007. Narratives 8, 9, 20, 21, 24, 33, 34, 35, and 36.

Jamir, N S & P Lal, "Ethnozoological practices among Naga Tribes", *Indian Journal of Traditional Knowledge*, Vol.4 (1), Jan. 2005, pp. 100-104.

Jamir, Rev. L. Pona. Oral narration. Mopongchuket village, May 24, 2008. Narratives 10, 15, and 16.

Jenkins, Richard, *Social Identity*, London: Routledge, 1996.

Lolenmayang, Aoli Longchar Liyonga Jajaba Lipok, Mokokchung: Aoli Longchar Mongdang, 2022.

Longchar, L. Teka. Oral narration. Longkhum village, June 13, 2008. Narrative 11.

Longchar, Longrichila. Oral narration. Longkhum village, December 20, 2007. Narratives 13, 22, 23, 30, and 40.

Longchar, Wati, Yangkllhao Vashum (eds.), *Traditional Tribal Worldview and Ecology*, Jorhat: Tribal Study Centre, ETC, 1998.

Longkumer, Anungla, *Folklore of Eastern Nagaland*, Department of Underdeveloped Areas (DUDA), Government of Nagaland, 2017.

Longkumer, Otsufuba. Oral narration. Longkhum village, December 18, 2007. Narratives 3, 4, 25, 26, 27, 31, 32, 37, 38, and 39.

Longkumer, Sakunungla. Oral narration. Longkhum village, June 18, 2008. Narratives 6, 18, and 19.

Longkumer, Tsükdinungba. Oral narration. Changtongya village, April 24, 2008. Narratives 2, 5, 7, 12, 17, and 28.

Maheo, Lorho Mary, *The Mao Naga Tribe of Manipur: A Demographic Anthropological Study*, New Delhi: Mittal Publications, 2004.

Mao, X.P., "The origin of Tiger, Spirit and Humankind: A Mao Naga Myth", NEHU, Shillong-22 *Indian Folklife*, Serial No.33, July 2009.

Mills, J.P., *The Ao Nagas*, Kohima, Directorate of Art and Culture, 1926.

Mongsen Mongdang, Report "*Mongsen Lipok Terajem Bushiba Osang*", 1985

Moustakas, C., *Heuristic research: Design, Methodology and Applications*, California: Sage Publications. 1990.

Ozukum, R. Nungshimeren. Oral narration. Mopongchuket village, June 26, 2008. Narrative 14.

Panger Imchen, *Ao Mongsen Lipok*, Mongsen Mongdang, Mokokchung, 1990.

Robb, Peter, "The Colonial State and Constructions of Indian Identity: An Example on the Northeast Frontier in the 1880s", *Modern Asian Studies*, Vol. 31, No. 2 (May), 1997, pp. 245-283.

Shakespear, L.W., *History of Upper Assam, Upper Burma and North East Frontier*, 1914.

Shimray, R.R. *Origin and Culture of Nagas*, New Delhi: Samsok Publications, 1985.

Smith, W.C, *The Ao-Naga Tribes of Assam*, New Delhi: Mittal Publications. (Reprinted), 2002.

Stets, Jan E., "Role Identities and Person Identities: Gender Identity, Mastery Identity, and Controlling One's partner" *Sociological Perspectives* 38, 1995, pp. 129–50.

Stracey, P.D. *Nagaland Nightmare*, Bombay: Allied Publishers, 1968.

William Nepuni, *Socio-Cultural History of Shüpfomei Naga Tribe: A Historical Study of Ememei, Lepaona, Chüluve and Paomata generally known as Mao-Poumai Naga tribe*, New Delhi: Mittal Publications, 2010

# INDEX

## A